Pimp My Fiction

Secrets of How to Write a Novel: Learn Writing Techniques
from Successful Authors of Creative Writing Guides

Writer's Resource Series

Paula Wynne

Prado Press
London, United Kingdom

Writers' Resource Series

A~Z Writers' Character Quirks: A~ Z of Behaviours, Foibles, Habits, Mannerisms & Quirks for Writers to Create Fictional Characters

&

101 Writers' Scene Settings: Unique Location Ideas & Sensory Details for Writers to Create Vivid Scene Settings

Pick up free chapters: http://eepurl.com/bSpEOv

More Books by This Author

Also by Paula Wynne
Create a Successful Website
Pimp My Site

Writers' Resource Series
Pimp My Fiction
A~Z of Writers' Character Quirks
101 Writers' Scene Settings

Torcal Trilogy
The Grotto's Secret – Published 2016
The Sacred Symbol – Due to be published 2016
The Lunar Legacy – Due to be published 2017

Author Contact & Copyright

Copyright © 2016 by Paula Wynne.

Paula Wynne/Prado Press

United Kingdom

www.paulawynne.com/contact

Pimp My Fiction/ Paula Wynne – 2nd edition

First Published 2015 by Prado Press

ISBN-13: 978-1530621743

ISBN-10: 1530621747

Cover Art: Kent Wynne

Editors: Betsy Smith

Book Layout: Slavisa Zivkovic

Dedication

To every aspiring novelist seeking knowledge to write their first bestseller

We are all apprentices in a craft where
no one ever becomes a master.
Ernest Hemingway

Contents

Foreword

During a clear-out, I stumbled across a shoe box crammed with 3.5" disks. My heart danced: These were the wonderful stories I had written fifteen years earlier and believed lost. Thrilled, I opened the files and settled down to read.

Oh dear! What predictable word choices, what shallow POV! How could I have thought this was good writing? At the time, I viewed those pieces as proud pillars of my accomplishment.

Comparing my writing then and now, I marvel at how much I've grown as a writer. I've learnt new skills, developed a strong author's voice, and gained a nuanced understanding of the craft.

Where I was once an apprentice and then a journeywoman, I've reached master level. And as with all trades, writing mastery is not a destination but a portal to further learning.

I didn't always see it this way. For many years, I wrote fiction in the belief that I knew it all and had to prove it. Success eluded me. Instead of acclaim, I garnered rejections - which in those days came in the form of pre-printed slips: 'We regret this submission doesn't meet our current requirements, and wish you luck placing it elsewhere.'

My breakthrough came when I changed my attitude and allowed myself to be simply a seeker with nothing to prove and a lot to learn - what Zen practitioners call 'beginner's mind'.

I identified the weaknesses of my writing - feeble plots, dragging pace and wordy style - and set about systematically upgrading my skills. Within months, this paid off. After years of spirit-sapping rejections, acceptances came rolling in. This wave of success has continued - with peaks and troughs - ever since.

Honing my craft to grow as a writer has become a joyful pursuit. Every year, I pick one area to improve, and work on it until my skill leaps to a high level.

For this, I've applied different learning strategies. I joined writers' groups and critique workshops, took adult education and online classes, analysed the works of famous authors and studied how-to-write books. I even went to university part time to earn a Master's degree in Creative Writing.

To my surprise, the most effective learning methods were the inexpensive ones. I learnt more from books than from the costly university education.

For writers who want to take their craft to the next level, books are ideal. You can find guides for almost any specialist skill you seek. Good books guide, inform, inspire, solve problems, encourage, empower or entertain.

Paula Wynne has compiled the books she found helpful on her journey, and her reviews can serve as your starting point. Which book is most useful for your work in progress? Which will help you most to grow as a writer? Which teaching style do you enjoy? Which aligns with your vision?

Modern publishing methods mean you can download the free samples of several promising books, or click the 'Look Inside' feature before you buy. Pick books which teach you what you want to learn, at your level, for your genre, and in a style you enjoy.

Keep in mind that nobody can tell you what you must write. Every writer and every story is different. Good guides don't make rules, they offer advice. It's your artistic responsibility to select influences which suit your vision.

For under £100 a year, you can get a college-level education, tailored to your interests. Put together your own programme of study, choose your major and supporting courses, and decide which assignments to write. You won't have to pay tuition fees, spend your precious time travelling to college or abide by someone else's schedule.

You can study full-time, part-time or in the brief periods between other commitments. You may decide to study dialogue this term, and plot structure next, or you may pick a new topic every month. Instead of formal assessments, you can invite constructive feedback from your peers.

Of course, you need to apply the techniques you learn to your writing. Pure theory won't make you an author. Write a lot. Try out many techniques and see how they work for you.

'Writing can't be taught,' some people claim. What they mean is that they can't teach it, or worse, that they can't - or don't want to - *learn*.

Unlike you. You've picked up this book because of your desire to learn new facets of your craft and to become the best writer you can possibly be. Enjoy your journey to mastery.

Rayne Hall

Introduction

It's none of their business that you have to learn to write.
Let them think you were born that way. ~ Ernest Hemingway

Some writing experts say a novelist's education is never complete. I believe that! For a long time, I have been obsessed with learning everything to improve my writing. I have acquired a bookshelf of excellent reference books by highly acclaimed authors.

Many of these books have changed my writing, so I wanted to share this list of exceptional books with other aspiring novelists.

These fantastic authors are never far from me as I travel on my writing journey, because I am constantly diving back into their books to remind myself of the powerful techniques they reveal.

More importantly, these books have taught me how to keep my readers intrigued so they stay up at night and keep turning the pages. I wholeheartedly admit that I want to worry my readers (Don't we all?) and have them desperate to find out what happens next.

One of my beta readers for my first novel, *The Grotto's Secret*, told me she was 'panting for breath at the end of each chapter.'

Wow! How cool is that for an aspiring author to hear?

Why This Odd Title?

One reason is because of my bestselling book on digital marketing. While writing the manuscript, I struggled with a title until one night I bolted upright and had: *Pimp My Site* in my head.

Not that I liked the word 'pimp,' mind. I grew up as a good church-going girl, and as with most people, that word was pretty offensive to me. But after the popular TV series *Pimp My Ride* became my son's favourite show on the box, I started getting used to the word. So, *Pimp My Fiction* matches my second book, in a strange way.

Another reason is because the word 'pimp' has lots of meanings. The Oxford Dictionary of English states:

Verb:[with obj.](informal)make(something)more showy or impressive: He pimped up the car with spoilers and twin-spoke 18-inch alloys.

For relevance to pimping your fiction, the meaning is this:

Verb: [with obj.] (informal) make (our books) more readable or impressive: She pimped her novel with excellent writing techniques and transformed it into a page-turning bestseller.

What This Book Isn't

This Book is not about promoting or marketing your novel. I am in the process of writing another book, in which I will share my on-the-hoof learning as I build my reader platform. It will also include information on how I started marketing my first novel long before I even finished the final draft. Sign up to my VIP news to find out free copies of that book when it's ready: www.paulawynne.com/vip-news

The list I have created here does not cover actual writing skills, such as perfecting your grammar and honing your art of using language to make your words flow. I imagine that when you first started writing, you armed yourself with style guides.

Neither does this list give you books about motivating yourself to write with writing prompts or exercises. Just because you are reading this I assume you are motivated enough to want to write great fiction.

Finally, this book is not about me making money. I am not earning commission from promoting any of these books. I don't give you affiliate links, I simply leave it up to you to find the books you may want to read in your favourite book store or on Amazon. I aim to offer *Pimp My Fiction* free on all eBook platforms and hopefully Amazon will price-match and give it to you for free as well. This may not happen for a few months so if you paid for the book and download the check lists in this book and then stay on my mailing list, I will send you the FREE updated version with the new books I am currently reviewing.

What This Book Is

Instead, *Pimp My Fiction* gives you a list of the best writing books and HOW they can improve your writing.

Let's face it, as aspiring novelists we have to learn from the pros, the authors who have been there and found success in their writing career. If we are to become successful we must emulate them and copy their techniques.

Of course, this can easily be done by reading the great writers in your genre. In fact, that is part and parcel of the learning-to-write process. Read good books and learn new tricks from flourishing authors.

The kind of writer you are will probably be much like me: someone who has written for a long time, and dreamed of seeing their novel published, but deep inside, you've known that your manuscript lacks that little something that will cause readers to fizz through it and rave about it.

This list of my personal choices of writing guides will definitely assist new authors with the craft of writing. I say this with confidence because I know without doubt that the knowledge I have gained from them has improved my novel writing.

If you have come across books that are not mentioned here and you feel they should be, do drop me a line via my website, paulawynne.com. I'll be happy to include your review of the book in any future revisions of *Pimp My Fiction.*

Before We Begin

I asked Rayne Hall to write the foreword because I feel highly inspired by all her practical advice. Each time I finish one of her books, I pounce straight into my manuscript and hone, hone, hone! I do this when I'm working on scary scenes, fight scenes, and vivid settings.

In fact, I have even used her fight scenes as a blueprint. I did this for my novel *The Grotto's Secret* as well as the sequel I am currently writing, *The Sacred Symbol.*

My beta readers, who read *The Grotto's Secret,* told me that the 'tunnel' scenes were their favourite parts. The formula was taken directly from Rayne's template, where she builds up to the climax of a fight scene.

Combine that technique with her advice on vivid settings and scary scenes, then combine it with the other books I mention in the chapter called "Blueprints," and a new author has their own template for a novel!

One of the books listed is Jessica Page Morrell's book *Between the Lines.* I thought I'd have a bit of fun with Jessica's review. Along with a listing about her book, I have sprinkled her inspiring advice 'between the lines' of other listings on similar topics. Don't skip over the 'quotes;' read them. They are there as advice and motivation to help your writing grow.

Would you like to learn how to write a novel using fiction writing techniques from the best guides on the craft of creative writing?

Good! Let's tuck into this list of books and start learning how to write a page turning novel...

The Craft of Writing

The greatest part of a writer's time is spent in reading, in order to write; a man will turn over half a library to make one book. ~ Samuel Johnson

The craft of writing an exciting novel that fascinates our readers is *knowing* how to make things happen on the page.

To entice our readers to turn pages and see what happens next, we have to find the most exciting way to tell our story. As aspiring writers, we need to learn how to write fiction and to perfect our writing craft with dynamic words to connect our plot and characters to our readers.

This writing skill is acquired over time. Along with reading books in the genre we are writing, a new novelist will also find success from the guidance of writing tutors who share their knowledge and experience by writing reference books.

We have to learn how to structure our story with strategically placed plot points. But just as important is knowing how to weave our character's arc into scenes so they drive the story forward.

When creating our characters, we have lots of personality templates and different archetypes to choose from, yet whichever route we choose, we have to be sure the characters we create are completely believable. This includes putting them on an emotional journey throughout the story.

Just as important, we must ensure each character speaks with their own distinctive tone in the dialogue they use when they interact with other characters.

Likewise, our villains must be real and reveal their character traits slowly, to worry our readers. By exploring character viewpoint, we're able to give our readers a thrilling experience with a powerful point of view.

Next, we must discover ways to captivate our readers within the first few pages of our novels and keep them riveted and hooked throughout. We do this by writing vivid settings as seen through our character's senses.

Whatever genre we are writing; we must always have the desire to learn writing fiction techniques from acclaimed authors. Whether our passion is writing thrillers, supernatural and paranormal, fantasy and science fiction or romance, or even children's books, there is something for everyone in this book.

Within the pages of *Pimp My Fiction* I have included writing reference books that offer templates and blueprints to help you to start creating your plot, building your characters and writing your novel.

So, if you're reading this book because you want to find out how to write a novel, this ultimate list of writing fiction technique books will provide you with all the tools you will possibly need.

Above all, *Pimp My Fiction* will inspire, inform, and enlighten aspiring authors.

Structure Your Novel

Always grab the reader by the throat in the first paragraph,
send your thumbs into his windpipe in the second, and hold him
against the wall until the end. ~ Paul O'Neil

Plotting and structuring a novel is like driving a car without driving lessons. Or like building a skyscraper on a shed's foundations.

Some writers go the route of a 'pants' author, and fly along by the seat of their pants with no plans or structure. Others take their time to craft out their story using one of the story structure concepts, and only then do they start writing.

Which are you? I was a 'pants' writer, but after reading so many exceptional books on the craft of writing, I have become a plotter.

Building a Solid Story Foundation

In her book, *Writing a Killer Thriller* (see this excellent book listed in the chapter on writing thrillers), Jodie Renner goes through various structural formats that you can use to create your story structure with its plot points. Jodie says that it's vital that as the author of your story, you need to underpin your plot to ensure reader satisfaction.

I have a list of books coming up that you can read to learn more about structuring your novel, but here are a few other methods you can investigate in the meantime:

3 Acts to Your Structure

One good place to start is a simple 3 Act Structure where you have a beginning, middle and end with lots of plot points within each act.

Wikipedia tells us this about the classical 3 Act Structure:

1. The first act usually provides exposition, which establishes the main characters, their relationships and the world they live in. Later in the first act, a dynamic incident occurs to confront the main character (the protagonist), whose attempts to deal with the incident lead to a second and more dramatic situation. This is known as the first turning point; it signals the end of the first act and ensures that life will never be the same for the protagonist. It also raises a dramatic question that will be answered during the climax of the story. The dramatic question should be framed in terms of the protagonist's call to action, (Will X recover the diamond? Will Y get the girl? Will Z capture the killer?). This is known as the inciting incident, or catalyst. As an example, the inciting incident in the 1972 film

The Godfather occurs approximately 40 minutes into the film, when Vito Corleone is shot.

Practise writing your story's dramatic question. Better yet, post it near your work space so you're constantly reminded of its focus.
~ Jessica Page Morrell

2. The second act, also referred to as 'rising action,' typically depicts the protagonist's attempt to resolve the problem initiated by the first turning point, only to find him- or herself in ever worsening situations. Part of the reason protagonists seem unable to resolve their problems is because they do not yet have the skills to deal with the forces of antagonism that confront them. They must not only learn new skills but, in order to deal with their predicament, they must arrive at a higher sense of awareness of who they are and what they are capable of which in turn changes who they are. This is referred to as character development, or a character arc. This usually cannot be achieved by the protagonists alone, so they are often aided and abetted by mentors and co-protagonists.

3. The third act features the resolution of the story and its subplots. The climax is the scene or sequence in which the main tensions of the story are brought to their most intense point and the dramatic question is answered, leaving the protagonist and other characters with a new sense of who they really are.

Poke around the internet on this subject because there are lots of good articles that expand on it and give it more depth than shown here.

For new writers it is certainly much easier to start with a basic structure that is easy to get your head around.

8 Point Story Arc

This all sounds extremely formulaic, but it doesn't have to be. Yes, having some kind of basic structure woven around your novel and plot threads is important, but they are meant to be flexible.

The 'Blueprints' chapter of this book provides templates for writing your novel, which are certain to show you a light at the end of the writing tunnel.

This 8 point arc was created by Nigel Watts, and it's a perfect tool for keeping your story on track. When you start a new novel, this template is a good exercise to guide you into writing up a very loose and basic idea of how your story is going to pan out.

You may find that your plot hits on all these points, and you'll feel great knowing that you're on the right track.

Nigel's eight points:

1. Stasis
2. Trigger
3. The quest
4. Surprise
5. Critical choice
6. Climax
7. Reversal
8. Resolution

If you make notes straight into a document which describes each stage, it is pretty easy to plot out your storyline. It acts almost like a synopsis of how your story progresses with character growth points.

Once you have established the basic plan, you can continue to add sub plots and any other notes into the eight stages as they come to you. This bare outline slowly builds into the skeleton of your novel.

In a moment I will provide you with a link that gives you a basic understanding of all eight points of Nigel's story arc. You can use this document as an outline, as I have described above.

12 Point Hero's Journey

Intrigued and fascinated by mythology, author Joseph Campbell studied the myths of many cultures. He claimed that nearly all myths, and some other story types, have similar ideas, and the heroes' adventures are almost identical in their format; they're just told from different characters' points of view in diverse plots.

He called the twelve stages of adventure the 'hero's journey.'

1. **Ordinary World:** This step refers to the hero's normal life at the start of the story, before the adventure begins.

2. **Call to Adventure:** The hero is faced with something that makes him begin his adventure. This might be a problem or a challenge he needs to overcome.

3. **Refusal of the Call:** The hero attempts to refuse the adventure because he is afraid.

4. **Meeting with the Mentor:** The hero encounters someone who can give him advice and ready him for the journey ahead.

5. **Crossing the First Threshold:** The hero leaves his ordinary world for the first time and crosses the threshold into adventure.

6. **Tests, Allies, Enemies:** The hero learns the rules of his new world. During this time, he endures tests of strength and will, meets friends, and comes face to face with foes.

7. **Approach:** Setbacks occur, sometimes causing the hero to try a new approach or adopt new ideas.

8. **Ordeal:** The hero experiences a major hurdle or obstacle, such as a life or death crisis.

9. **Reward:** After surviving death, the hero earns his reward or accomplishes his goal.

10. **The Road Back:** The hero begins his journey back to his ordinary life.

11. **Resurrection Hero:** The hero faces a final test where everything is at stake and he must use everything he has learned.

12. **Return with Elixir:** The hero brings his knowledge or the "elixir" back to the ordinary world, where he applies it to help all who remain there.

A quick internet search will also give you a visual reference that shows you the stages in diagrams.

Uniting Story Structure and Character Arc

Michael Hauge goes one step further by saying the best heroes must achieve two compelling goals: an outer journey of accomplishment; and a deeper, inner journey of transformation and fulfillment. Again, a Google search will show you how Michael presents his unique approach to mastering these two essential components of your story.

Your task as a fiction writer is to create a dramatic and interesting conflict that operates in the outside world, but also draws from a deep vein within your protagonist, possibly based on their greatest fear. ~ Jessica Page Morrell

If you're stuck for time and you want to jump ahead, you can download Michael's inner and outer journey diagram, along with his explanation to the six stages to a well-structured story here: http://eepurl.com/bC_vjX

When you go to this link you will get the following documents in Word that you can use to create your story structure:

1. Michael Hauge's inner and outer journey diagram
2. His explanation to the six stages to a well-structured story
3. A basic outline of Nigel Watt's eight-point story arc
4. My infographic on writing a thriller
5. A surprise – coming up soon …

And don't forget the juicy bits we have coming up in the chapter on blueprints. But before we get there, let's look at some excellent writing books that will teach you more about plotting your story with a good, solid structure.

Plot and Structure

By James Scott Bell

As one of my favourite writing tutors, James comes up trumps once again. His writing guide, *Plot and Structure*, helps aspiring novelists like you and me with techniques for crafting a plot that will grip your readers from start to finish.

How does plot influence story structure? What's the difference between plotting for commercial and literary fiction? How do you revise a plot or structure that's gone off course?

James Scott Bell gives you techniques for crafting strong beginnings, middles and ends with easy to understand plotting diagrams and charts. He explains how to brainstorm to be sure that your plot ideas are original, and you are able to fix plot problems as and when they arise in your novel.

Using Plot Points in Your Novel

Some other authors of writing reference guides use the terms 'incidents' or 'plot points,' to describe the first incident that turns your story and points your character on another route. James, however, talks about doorways. Your character must go through certain 'doorways' to get from the beginning of the story to the middle, and then another 'doorway' to get to the end of the story.

He also draws you further into plotting your novel or thriller ideas by finding ways for your readers to bond with your fictional characters, making emotional connections through stimuli such as empathy, sympathy, hardship and jeopardy.

A good plot is about disturbance to a character's inner and outer lives. ~ James Scott Bell

Additionally, James goes into great detail about plotting for your story beginning, the middle and the end and re-iterates what so many writing experts advise – stretch out the tension and raise the stakes so that your character is facing some type of grave peril. If lots of bad things are not happening to your fictional people, your story is going to be boring and unreadable. As my writing mentor once told me, you have to throw stones at them.

James also reminds us to say over and over to ourselves –Who cares? Is there enough going on for the reader to care about what happens? What does the lead character stand to lose if he doesn't solve the central problem of the story? More importantly, is that enough? Remember –Who cares?!

Write Powerful Evocative Scenes

Scenes are the essential building blocks of plot; we use scenes to illustrate and dramatise those disturbances. On the subject of scenes, James says that if we as novelists can make each of our scenes truly memorable, we will have written a novel that is unforgettable.

According to James, an emotional scene is fresh and surprising and emotionally intense. It involves characters we care about doing things that we feel absolutely compelled to watch or read about. You create unforgettable scenes by recharging what is forgettable, making the scenes come alive with tension and originality.

He goes on to explain that most often, the best way to create this unforgettable scene is to intensify the conflict. Two characters oppose each other; they have the strongest imaginable reasons for doing so.

As far as James is concerned, the four areas of a scene include action, reaction, set-up and deepening. He goes into greater detail about each of these in turn, but I don't want to give away all his secrets.

Hook Readers into Your Scenes

I also like the way James brings some HIP into scenes with Hook, Intensity and Prompt (HIP).

Hook: grab the readers' attention from the word go and pull them into the narrative/story.

Intensity: pack your scenes with tension primarily through conflict and as your story builds, increase the intensity of that tension and conflict. If it isn't strong enough, ratchet it up. If there is no tension and conflict, delete the scene. Design every scene to vary in emotional intensity, and keep the level of tension shifting around. Time the events in your novel so that the most vivid part of the narrative stands out as the point where you want the reader to feel the greatest emotion.

Prompt: end scenes with a prompt to make readers turn the page. There are many great read-on prompts, such as a secret suddenly revealed, a mysterious line of dialogue, a big decision, a question left hanging and one of the best ones to use is impending danger. Dean Koontz does this so well – all you need to do is read one of his books to find a master at using impending danger to keep you turning his pages.

Opening Lines

James also tells us that opening lines must hook a reader. Open any Dean Koontz novel, and you will find an excellent example of one line paragraphs with a named person and some sort of immediate interruption to normality. Not just anything, something dangerous or ominous. An interruption to normal life. Give readers a feeling of motion, of something happening or about to happen from the absolute first line.

Look at this example from Dean Koontz's *Darkfall*:

Penny Dawson woke and heard something moving furtively in the dark bedroom.

Yikes! Dean simultaneously introduces the character we are going to root for and slides in this delicious hook so that we have to read on to find out who or what is moving in the dark.

Fiction is about characters that readers are intimately involved with and worried about. ~ Jessica Page Morrell

James finishes his *Plot and Structure* with a list of tried and tested plot themes, such as 'The Quest,' and he explains each one in turn; for example: rudiments of the quest and structure of the quest.

There are lots more plot patterns, so be sure to read this great book by a master at the craft of teaching novelists how to write great fiction. You will learn so much about plotting your novel with structure.

Who knows, with great writing books like this, maybe you and I will write great novels one day soon!

Scene & Structure

By Jack Bickham

I've often confessed that I am obsessed with reading writing guides to help me (and other authors) to create a page-turning novel that has readers staying up late at night because they simply can't stop reading.

Any aspiring writer who has every intention of self-publishing their book simply has to read Jack's *Elements of Fiction Writing - Scene & Structure* by the fantastic publisher of writing resource books, *Writers Digest.*

Not only will this great writing guide teach you how to hook your readers and how to structure your story, scene by scene, but most importantly, it will teach you how to worry your readers.

Worry Readers with Worry Plates

For me, *Scene & Structure* has been paramount in learning how to worry my readers. Jack teaches you how to 'worry' your readers into following your story to the end, how to prolong your main character's struggle while moving the story ahead and how to juggle cause and effect to create your story action.

BINGO! Jack makes us novelists think of ourselves as jugglers. When you spot a juggler busking on the street, you will see that a crowd has gathered around him. That crowd is probably oohing and aahing. Why? Because they are worried about what the juggler will drop.

If there were two jugglers, one with rubber balls up in the air and the other tossing plates into his juggling mix - which would you watch and worry about? The rubber ball juggler can miss a trick and the ball will simply drop and bounce away. No worries.

Whereas the plate juggler will have his audience in twisted knots because they are frantic that his plates will come crashing down.

That's what Jack is teaching us writers to do. To juggle worry plates! In your own juggling act when you're writing your page-turning novel, don't juggle anything other than plates.

Go through your novel and ensure that you throw 'worry plates' into the air in each chapter. Don't throw them on the floor like Greek

Dancers do and don't think that they can come crashing down after you've thrown them into a chapter. They can't!

You have to keep the plates in the air so that your readers will stay worried all the way through your novel. That's what Jack is teaching you to do in this excellent writing guide.

If you can only afford one writing guide to improve your writing this year, it has to be *Scene & Structure*. Without doubt.

Do yourself the biggest favour and go get *Scene & Structure* by Jack Bickham now!

Plot versus Character

By Jeff Gerke

This is another book on my shelf that teases me with all its Post-It notes. Looking at the table of contents you will see the book is divided into three parts: Memorable Characters, Marvellous Plots and Plot and Character.

It seems odd to have a book with the word 'character' in the title under a section about story structure. That's because this book shows you how a story can be driven by either the plot or the character.

Jeff starts by explaining the difference between character-first writers and plot-first writers. He gives the ups and downs of each and shows how, no matter which type you are, you can marry the two together.

Plotting means you're dramatising your character arc through a series of events, reversals and problems, while keeping the pace and speed at which the story unfolds firmly in check. ~ Jessica Page Morrell

In the 'characters' section, Jeff goes into detail about core personality types and delves into their inner journey. He discovers the 'knot,' the 'moment of truth' and the 'inciting incident,' along with other topics that pave a character's journey through a story.

When you get into the section on plot, you'll work through the three-act structure and why each act is important to your storyline.

Finally, Jeff shows you how you can integrate being a character-first writer or a plot-first writer. And how plot and character together represent the beginning of a beautiful friendship.

Structure Your Novel

By K.M. Weiland

Katie's writing guide *Structuring Your Novel: Essential Keys for Writing an Outstanding Story* is an easy to read and understand resource on story structure.

In my obsession to write a page-turning novel that has my readers on the edge of their seat, I am always on the hunt for excellent writing guides. *Structuring your Novel* is part and parcel of creating a riveting read so when you open Katie's book on *Structuring Your Novel*, you'll find it opens with a bang and explains how to hook your reader with a riveting first line.

There are five elements to this, and Katie explains them in detail. And then she shows you examples from film and fiction so you can see the five elements in action.

Many writers write a full manuscript, and even when they're finished, don't know where to begin their story. Katie covers this with topics such as character, action, setting, 'in Media Res' and how to create your book's dramatic question.

Your Book's Dramatic Question

As Katie explains, 'The Dramatic Question' is where a question is posed at the beginning of the book, and the ending answers it. If the ending fails to answer the specific question set out in the beginning, the whole book will fail.

What will be revealed in the ending is the answer to your story's dramatic question. It's this one issue that will fuel the entirety of your plot. This is vitally important because once you've set up a powerful question in your story's opening, you are obligated to follow through by purposefully answering it in the final pages. Setting up your book to allow your reader to discover that answer in the story's ending is the only way to create continuity and resonance.

In *Structuring Your Novel,* I found the 'Five Elements of a Riveting First Line' so important to my own writing that I typed up a check-list so that when I am starting or finishing a book, I can go back and double check that I have captured these 'riveting' elements in my own opening.

With each section of valuable learning, Katie gives you 'Takeaway Value' where she summarises the main points by firing a few bullets at you to be sure you got the message!

Writers who spend many hours planning and plotting their story and writing up a story structure know the value of plot points and at what stages they should be incorporated. If you've done your homework on plotting your story, you'll know that the story is divvied up into 3 main sections: Beginning, Middle and End.

The important scenes (called set pieces), where emotional payoffs occur, should be scattered throughout the course of your story. ~ Jessica Page Morrell

It's learning how to get those plot points into action at the right stages that ultimately pushes your reader on and keeps them hooked and reading. Here Katie explains the different plot points, where they should be positioned and why. She follows through on her advice by giving you examples from popular fiction so you can see where other successful authors have plugged in their plot points and how it has shot their story forward.

Between The Lines

By Jessica Page Morrell

As I said in the introduction, I thought I'd have a bit of fun with Jessica's review. Up to this point you will have seen inspiring quotes from her book sprinkled 'between the lines' of other listings, and you'll see many more on different topics.

By opening the pages of Jessica's book you'll quickly see what she means by writing between the lines. To keep your readers spellbound, you need to apply subtle writing techniques.

In Jessica's first sentence she says, 'The best fiction touches the deep layers in us. A writer achieves this by embedding dozens of practical skills into their stories.' The process, she says, is artful and often sly. It is not merely a matter of employing tricks. Fiction writing means applying craft and artifice, and it can be learned. And Jessica goes into great detail to teach you how to develop and use this skill.

Your reader wants to be lured from his daily life into your story. He wants to forget his bank balance, bad back and upcoming dentist appointment. He wants to travel somewhere, be someone else, feel what your character feels and know what your characters know. This emotional involvement comes from your reader believing in your story world from the opening lines.

Jessica starts by giving you nine essential ingredients of all successful novels. Study these, as they are vital to your own success as a novelist. If any of these components are missing in your story, go back to it and make sure you get them in there.

After delving into the art of keeping your readers spellbound, she dips into the topic of 'backstory' and shows you how to weave any history between the lines rather than just creating an info dump. Use Jessica's ideas to reveal the important information at the right moments.

Even if your story has a quiet theme or a languid pace, Jessica states that it still must be a gripping, irresistible page-turner. She goes on to explain lots of techniques and devices that will press your story ahead and create narrative drive.

Whether it be a subtle or bold brush stroke, Jessica arms you with the knowledge of structural devices to move the action forward and raise questions or cause curiosity about things to come. Thrusters and cliff-hangers are part of driving your readers to turn the page, despite it being well beyond their bed time, and Jessica shows you how to deploy such devices.

Topics such as imagery and charms, sense of place and sensory surround ensures you are creating a powerful world seen through your character's eyes. Moving to the subjects of foreshadowing, pacing, tension and suspense teaches you to keep your reader involved in your plot and subplot.

Jessica also covers other areas such as theme and premise, epilogues and prologues and transitions.

There is so much advice in this book, you will need lots of time to absorb it all and distribute it throughout your manuscript. That's why I am keeping this listing short so that I can impart some of the potent tips from Jessica 'between the lines' of the rest of this book ...

Writing the Picture

By Robin U Russin and William Missouri Downs

This book is classed as a screen writing book, but its contents reflect everything a writer should know about story development.

On opening it, you will find chapters on how to impress your reader, theme and emotions, the world of your story, characters and much, much more.

Although it does give directions on how to write a screenplay format with things like beats and sequences, many of those writing elements can be carried into your novel writing.

My copy of the book has lots of coloured markers sticking out, reminding me where to hop in and out when I need inspiration on writing pictures rather than words. I love how the authors describe how to introduce your characters. For example: Sam is a handsome man in spite of the burn marks on his cheeks. Or: Age is catching up on pretty Sally. And: Judd, a tall, yet drooping basketball player. All of these quick descriptions give your reader immediate pictures in their minds. Isn't that what we're supposed to do as writers?

Robin and William do the same for describing locations. Here they give a great example of a Victorian room:

A faded shell of its former glory. Thin sunset light leeches through the crud on the cracked windows. In the shadows sits Spike, the family dog, fangs bared. But he's dead and dusty. Stuffed, like the furniture.

What an incredible picture that creates in your mind. Just from using picture-making words! The authors explain that to do this we must appeal to the senses and use words that place specific words in the reader's imagination.

The best verbs create pictures in your reader's mind and sound like what they mean. ~ Jessica Page Morrell

Strong descriptions allow readers to see, hear, smell and feel. They get satisfaction from creating their own mental pictures and drawing on their own memories, but it is our job as authors to guide them.

This is another book that gives you templates for creating heroes; it covers different archetypes and the various stages of their journey, such as their call to adventure (also known as the inciting incident).

The Writer's Journey

By Christopher Vogler

This is one of the first books on story structure I read. If you want to use mythic structure to create powerful stories, this book gives you step-by-step guidelines to blend with the knowledge you gained from the other books listed above.

I read the original version published way back in 1999, but Vogler has written a new edition that is said to reawaken established writers and inspire a new generation of writers with fresh insights on creating great stories.

The version I read showed me the inner workings of stories. The newer edition should also give insight into the ancient and deep-seated patterns of emotion that speak to us through the symbolic language of myth.

It applies the classic principles of Joseph Campbell's 'The Hero's Journey' to modern storytelling. I must get around to reading all Joseph's updates.

The 12 Pillars of Novel Construction

By CS Lakin

Susanne jumps into the fray on novel structure by explaining the essentials a builder would need before he started constructing a house ... or any building for that matter.

In a similar fashion, authors need to get their tools gathered and ready for a new project before they begin. This is where Susanne's help comes into play. She offers you twelve pillars, but starts with the four most essential pillars which will be 'corners' for your novel.

Imagine constructing a square without one of its corners. It's not a square any more. Better still, get out your kid's Lego blocks and set four of them out on the carpet and then add another layer of Lego bricks on top. Now pull out one of the four corners.

Collapse!

That's exactly what Susanne is showing us writers. Our novels will collapse if we don't have the essential 'bricks' in place.

Brick Up Your Novel

Susanne's four corner pillars are:

1. Concept with a kicker
2. Protagonist with a goal
3. Conflict with high stakes
4. Theme with heart

Your entire novel will be built on these corner pillars. Each corner brick is moulded and fired by the same hands that will construct the next corner stone. By this I mean, as you work on each corner pillar, plotting, researching and planning your story, you shape each 'corner' in such a way that they all connect the story.

Conflict is anything that stands in the way of your character reaching her goal. ~ CS Lakin

If you have no idea what I'm rattling on about, no fear, Susanne explains each corner in great detail so when you get to the fourth pillar you can see your story's square and how these parts are essential construction tools.

The first pillar Susanne explains as a kick-ass high concept. But what is high concept? Quite simply, your story concept has to be strong enough to draw an audience of readers without any other components. It is simply the story idea alone that will promise an emotional experience.

Kick Your Novel's Butt

Susanne goes on to show how adding a kicker to your high concept will turn it into a WOW novel that readers will talk about for a long time.

Susanne explains that:

- Kickers make readers ask questions they want answered
- Kickers move ordinary into extraordinary
- Kickers take ordinary ideas and put them on steroids

This accomplished author of umpteen novels doesn't just tell, she shows. First she tells you what each corner pillar is and then goes on to show you how to construct them and build them in your fiction.

Corner Stone Checklist

I had already written *The Grotto's Secret* (which was in the middle of it's second edit) when I read Susanne's 12 Pillars so I noted the four pillars and beside each one I wrote the corners of my novel. Phew, I was relieved to find I had the corners in place. But even so, I still went back into the manuscript and added ideas that came to me. Thankfully, my editor is flexible and didn't mind me adding in new chunks of text to strengthen my novel's foundation.

Building More Blocks

So when all four pillars are in place you can move onto the next important eight pillars of constructing your story.

Or like me you may already have a finished story in place where you can go through Susanne's twelve pillars to ensure your corner stones are in place.

Conflict must include high stakes ~ what is risked or threatened must be precious to your character. ~ CS Lakin

Ideally, you'd start a novel with this kind of knowledge in your construction kit bag, but it can easily be applied to an existing story.

I am just constructing the second novel in my Torcal Trilogy, *The Sacred Symbol*, and I have downloaded the cheat sheets Susanne gives you at the end of each pillar. Using these as templates I will be carving my four corner bricks into place before I work on the next eight pillars. I won't do a spoiler here and tell you about those, except to say that you can work on the pillars in any order. Clearly, the first four corner pillars will be the first place you start digging up trenches to build your novel's foundations, but once those are in place (even in rough format) you can start working on the other pillars.

You can also try Susanne's brainstorming methods where one central theme turns into a treasure trove of ideas for scenes adding conflict and tension.

High stakes are about what your character cares passionately about. ~ CS Lakin

Building Your Premise

The interesting thing about Susanne's corner pillars is that when you come to write your novel's premise, which is your one line story concept, you will be focusing on your concept (first corner pillar) and detailing your protagonist and their goal (second pillar) along with the conflict and high stakes (third pillar) that make your story compelling to the reader. Adding the story theme in a subtle way (fourth pillar) will enhance your premise and make readers want to rush out and get your book.

Like many other books I have listed in *Pimp My Fiction*, Susanne's *12 Pillars of Novel Construction* can be slotted into other chapters because it covers characters, tension, scenes, settings and so much more. Hop over to the chapter on Blueprints to see how Susanne's pillars will underpin your novel's template.

Builder's Kit Bag

I'm getting this mental image - a builder's leather belt around my waist with many pockets. The largest pocket right up front is for construction tools. In that pocket is all this knowledge we've covered so far on structuring novels and plotting scenes that worry our readers.

So what's in all the other pockets? Ooh, many more delicious tools for authors. When you've finished reading *Pimp My Fiction*, your kit belt-bag will be stuffed with all the knowledge and learning you need to get your novel written!

Take Off Your Pants

By Libbie Hawker

Libbie starts by asking: Are you a plotter or a pantser?

Plotters plan and research their storylines in great depth before starting the first chapter, while pantser's write by the seat of their pants.

Libbie aims to teach writers one important thing: To outline your books for faster and better writing. The method she presents in this book isn't the only way to plot out a book, nor is it is the type of plot structure the only form a story can take.

Libbie isn't going to dictate the one true story structure, or to decree that all works of fiction share these same qualities. She simply wants to share her own personal organisational methods that have dramatically increased her speed and efficiency as a writer.

The key benefit to you as an aspiring novel is that it allows you to analyse a book's commercial appeal before you begin to write, thus saving you time and helping you build your writing with speed and efficiency.

If you don't follow a planned routine with your writing, you can't go wrong reading this book, it covers all aspects of writing, from characterisation to plot and story structure to pacing your novel.

How to Fix Your Novel

By Steve Alcorn

Once you open this book and see the contents, you'll dive into the first chapter. Steve advocates that great fiction is built on a three act structure that balances action and emotion.

From the details in this chapter on structuring your novel you can see that a good story foundation is your key to success. Steve believes in this so much that he has a large section of his book dedicated to showing you how the three different acts work, what triggers each plot point and how it effects the rest of the story.

You can use this as a template, along with the others mentioned in the chapter on 'Blueprints' whereby you follow his guidance and plan your story within his three acts checkpoints. By doing this you will be guaranteed a story that works dramatically.

Equally important to Steve is how to make your plot really grab readers' attention with conflict, suspense and mystery. He covers these important subjects in detail, along with ensuring your fictional people have great dialogue, both internal and external.

What I love most about Steve's book is that it is easy to read and quite addict-able. You go through the advice with ease and understand what Steve is explaining without having to stop and digest it.

For example, he breaks down the difference between plot and story so effectively that you get it straight away. More than that, he refers to it several times in the book to show you again and again how important it is to know that the plot drives your novel forward with physical actions, while the story is your character's emotional journey.

By explaining the dramatic elements and how they make up a novel, you can quickly see that you need to have these elements in place in your novel before you continue.

Steve's book is such a smooth path: from the understanding of plot versus story, to having the dramatic elements in place, and then moving to character building and how to get your acts together.

If you're just starting to write a novel, this book has to be your first port of call!

Look Out For ...

When you get to the chapter on creating characters, you'll find Jeff Gerke's book *Plot Versus Character*. Although essentially a book on how plot and character work in unison to create your storyline, he also goes through the three-act structure.

When you get to the chapter on 'Writing for Children,' look out for the online course I took. The sections on structuring your novel are extremely thorough so that this Young Adult Fiction Writing Workshop would be great for aspiring novelists and writers for audiences of any age. You will learn a structure that will keep your readers turning the pages!

Most importantly, there is something so thrilling at the end of this book: your very own blueprints. Jack Bickham's book *Scene & Structure* is one of those. If you have an immediate need for a blueprint to write your novel, I invite you to hop to the end and peep at how *Scene & Structure* gives you the perfect plan for writing your novel. Otherwise, stay tuned, and you'll get to the blueprints soon enough.

Lots of information on Michael Hauge's six plot structure is widely available on the internet. Click the link below to download a diagram showing the character's arc, their inner and outer journey in addition to the six plot structure. You will also find explanations of how Hauge's six plot structure works. Download it here: http://eepurl.com/bC_vjX

Your First Few Pages

Remember, begin with tension and immediacy. Make readers feel the story has started. They want to be in your world, not be told about it. Don't preface - plunge in. ~ Jerome Stern, Making Shapely Fiction

The First 50 Pages

By Jeff Gerke

Your novel's first 50 pages are vital to your success as an author. Jeff's *The First 50 Pages* is amongst the best writing reference books I have read.

My copy is littered with different coloured Post it notes sticking out the side for a quick jump back into it at any time. Why one of the best books? Oh dear, where do I begin? It's the kind of book you want to read and re-read and re-read. You want to force every sentence to stay permanently fixed in your writing mind.

Okay, I'll begin by saying this book is intended to help all aspiring novelists and writers and authors to hook both their reader and a potential publisher in the first 50 pages. That said, it has plenty of writing advice for your whole novel or scriptwriting project, not just a mere 50 pages.

Compelling opening scenes are the key to catching an agent or editor's attention and, of course, they are crucial to keeping your reader … well, reading.

Jeff sets out to ensure you know to begin your novel with the skill and intention to land you a book deal and keep readers' eyes glued to every page. But he doesn't just do that. He also arms any wannabe novelist with all the fire-power to create a page-turning story.

This writing tutor divided *The First 50 Pages* into two parts. The first half gets you inside the head of the first people who will encounter your opening pages – editors and agents –so you have an idea what factors are going to convince them to decide to give you a writing contract. And of course, if your readers are hooked at the start, they are much more likely to continue reading.

Secondly, Jeff provides you with insight into what you must accomplish in your first 50 pages in order to pull this off. He goes into great detail with important little things like beats and dialogue, and beats to break up dialogue.

Jeff goes on to explain why it's important to have characters in action or not in action in your opening pages, as well as the dos and don'ts of things like flashbacks and show and tell.

So many good writing reference books contain explanations about conflict, and Jeff stands by its importance, saying quite simply: no conflict, no publication.

Fiction Is Conflict

Not only agents and publishers are looking for stakes; your readers will also be watching for them. Later in the book, Jeff explains several ways to up the ante so your reader will start to care about your hero from page 1!

Jeff uses lots of movie examples – for good reason – to help you see in your mind's eye the visual aspects that will help with your story improvement. In other words, your writing should place your reader inside a vivid descriptive scene, much like placing someone in front of a camera and actually recording what they are doing rather than trying to tell someone (such as a reader) about it.

Telling is when you stop the story to explain something the reader is not very likely to care about. So why do it? This excellent writing teacher teaches you to reveal info through showing, thus advancing your story while revealing character traits.

Jeff's cool tool is to always ask yourself in a scene, 'Can the camera see it?'

For point of view Jeff says – one head at a time, so pick a head and stay in it. You need to master this idea in your first 50 pages and then stay with it to the end.

Engage Your Reader

Job 1 is to engage your reader, so part 2 of the book, which starts at page 60, begins with activating a ticking bomb. You set up your character's flaws or knots to show us how it is affecting him or her from the outset.

Part 2 is the truly engaging part, jammed and crammed with so many excellent teaching points, from introducing your characters and establishing their worlds to the one-act play and 3 act structure.

Start with the moment that changes the character's life forever. Or throw the reader right into the middle of action using all their senses. It's all about action, reaction and pace. ~ Joe Moore

This author explains how organising your work of fiction can benefit this story-telling framework, which ensures that you have included all the necessary pieces for a comprehensive narrative construction. I read another writing reference guide on this a few years ago and use this myself when constructing my stories.

I also loved chapter 12 and I was so hugely inspired, my brain went into overdrive as the gems rolled off the pages and I instantly found the solution to a problem in one of my novels that had been nagging at me for a long time.

Along with pages of detail, your 1st line and what makes it engaging, and showing the book's tone with the 'right hook,' Jeff also advises you on several ways you can begin your book.

Should it be prologue, hero action, in media res or in frame device? This is where I found my own resolution and rushed off to rewrite my beginning.

> *The first sentence can't be written until the final sentence is written.* ~ *Joyce Carol Oates*

No matter what, no matter how, no matter when, every – I say again – *every* novelist has to have a copy of Jeff's *The First 50 Pages* right beside their writing pad or laptop!

To dive in and out of, to remind themselves about 50 pages of wisdom, to get inspiration, to learn. All of that.

Go now and get it before you pick up your writing pen or set fingers to the keyboard. Go now! Nothing more needs to be said ...

Captivate Your Readers

By Jodie Renner

I found Jodie's exceptional *Writing a Killer Thriller* stuffed to the gills with short, sharp paragraphs giving vital advice to thriller writers like me. So compelling and easy to read, it was exactly the page turner that Jodie was advising her readers to create for their own thrillers.

Needless to say, when I spotted *Captivate Your Readers*, I suspected it would be similar to a really well-written thriller.

I wasn't wrong.

Firstly, I must give you a warning. Don't have Jodie's book arrive when you have a family weekend of outings and guests planned. The two will clash because *Captivate Your Readers* is like a magnet and will have you sneaking off at every spare moment to read it. When my copy arrived I didn't want to do anything except put my feet up and curl up beside the fire to read and learn from this editing expert. So I did!

Bring Fiction to Life

Jodie's book states that you will learn techniques to really bring your fiction to life for the readers, so they feel as if they're right there, on the edge of their seats, struggling along with the hero or heroine. The techniques she recommends will have readers staying up late at night, worrying, glued to the pages.

As writers, and especially self-published writers, we all want and need that kind of response from our readers.

I was intrigued that Jodie's book claimed to provide specific advice, with examples, for captivating readers and immersing them in your story world.

This book is an excellent example of practising what you preach. Jodie's skill - making you, the reader of her writing book, turn the pages – is proof that her techniques are bound to work for your books.

Just looking inside the book at the contents shows you that you will be consuming valuable information that every aspiring author needs to know, learn and practise in their own writing.

Page Turning Techniques

Again, the chapters are broken up into segments with lots of gripping headings, titled so that you automatically leap straight from one topic into the next and the next and the next. Along with these captivating headings, you have equally valuable subheadings, real examples of each piece of guidance with before and after examples so that you get a flavour of how you can improve your self-published manuscript. To top it all, a variety of bulleted lists will drive you from cover to cover.

When Jodie says she wants to teach you to *Captivate Your Readers,* believe her. Every page gives you ways to engage your reader by fostering a direct connection to the characters. Jodie goes into detail about doing this through deep point of view, showing instead of telling, avoiding author intrusions, and letting the characters tell the story. Jodie's book shows you how to provide the emotional involvement and immediacy that readers crave in fiction.

According to Jodie, you find the 'show, don't tell' mantra in all writing advice. Why? Because it's a critical concept to master if you want to engage your readers, get their heart rate quickening and keep them turning the pages.

I read this book in a couple of sittings, as I am sure you will do. Once you have read the final page, you will also realise that Jodie is applying just what she is teaching. Her writing guide races along at an electric pace, so hopefully these tips and tricks will creep into your own writing and set your fiction on fire.

Experience Scenes as the Reader

Your goal should be to put the reader right there in every scene to experience the action along with the characters. Jodie goes into fine detail about how to do this with dialogue, thoughts, actions and reactions. She also says that we must show every tiny movement in order to increase tension, suspense and intrigue. To draw out crucial scenes it's important to milk them for all they're worth.

Something important for all writers and authors to learn is deep point of view writing. Jodie explains this with examples of how to let your viewpoint character's mood and attitudes and observations (on other characters, setting) colour your descriptions and explanations in a scene. This way your novel comes alive, and your readers find they have entered a fascinating story world with an up close and personal read.

Sensory Writing

Sensory writing is critical to ensure that you captivate your reader. According to Jodie and many other expert writing coaches, using sights, sounds, scents, touch and taste from the character's point of view draws your reader deeper into the story. They are able to see, smell, taste, hear and feel along with your characters. This goes for thoughts and reactions too.

This is one of those books where you will occasionally jump in and out looking for that gold nugget of advice you know is there. I use sticky notes and have them sticking out of the book for easy reference, sky-diving me straight back to where I know I'll find the gold dust sprinkled over the page.

Look Out For …

Look back at *Plot and Structure* to remind yourself how James Scott Bell tells us that opening lines must hook a reader. And revisit his HIP formula.

Creating Characters

I try to create sympathy for my characters, then turn the monsters loose. ~ Stephen King

Think of Scarlett O' Hara from *Gone With The Wind* or Scout Finch from To *Kill A Mockingbird*. They never lived and they'll never die. Yet Margaret Mitchell and Harper Lee made their characters so believable they became immortal.

When building fictional characters we need to create characters who think, love, hope, cry, feel pain and even inflict pain.

As an aspiring author, or even a published novelist, you are always working towards building convincing characters for your stories and novels.

Building Believable Characters

By Marc McCutcheon

Marc starts by conducting an inspiring and informative round table where six novelists reveal their approaches to characterisation. Next, he provides a character questionnaire more detailed than the nosiest survey you can think of that you can use to flesh out the fictional people in your novels and stories.

The best part is still to come, and this is where you really start getting to the nitty gritty of your characters: Marc provides a thesaurus of human characteristics.

He's built this index in such a way that you can artfully fit both the physical characteristics and the psychological characteristics together so that your characters will seem to climb off the pages.

You'll learn how to describe the appearance of your characters from their eye shape and facial features, their hair and hairline, right to their body type and even their voice and tone. You may want to give your antagonist a low slung chest or jutting cones. Who knows?

But you won't and don't stop there. Along with their facial features come expressions: anger, happiness, surprise, pain, guilt, arrogance and don't forget lust. Will their face flush when they're embarrassed? Will they sniff their glass of cabernet like a connoisseur?

Maybe they'll walk around with a wounded look in their eyes. With each expression, Marc arms you with body language responses. What more could you want?

And you don't just put clothes on your characters, you need to consider giving them a certain style – or no style at all, for that matter.

Their style, or absolute lack of it, will determine how they dress and what they dress in, whether it be old tacky pants and sweaters, or fitted jackets and suits. Will they wear slinky low cut dresses or corduroys or cargos? Maybe they'll accessorize their outfits with hats, shoes and glasses that match their clothing. There are so many possibilities for a writer to choose from!

First, find out what your hero wants, then just follow him! ~ Ray Bradbury

Then you'll get cracking on their personality, give them vices and ailments or hobbies and sports and decide if they have an occupation that could give you added plot points. You can even decide if they have memberships of a club or association, such as a mountaineering club.

And will a condition such as the episodic harsh breathing of asthma speed along your story plot? Someone who belongs to a mountaineering club, yet suffers from asthma? Interesting!

You'll need to spice up those little details that make or break a character like giving them a speech mannerism such as a lazy drawl.

Whatever you do with building your own believable characters, if you're determined to be a published novelist [like me] you need this book on your writing reference book shelf, right beside your writing chair, so you can dive in and out as you please.

Ideally, you'll spend lots of time with your nose in Marc's thesaurus but it is the kind of book you can get in and out of as quickly or as leisurely as you see fit.

Breathing Life into Characters

By Rachel Ballon

No matter the genre, your characters must be realistic and credible in order for your fiction to work. We know that for a hard-core fact. In this series of building believable characters, we are determined to arm you with the knowledge and characteristics of human nature.

Rachel Ballon [PhD] helps us with her book, *Breathing Life into Your Characters*, by giving you information about human nature, but she goes even further by detailing various mental health issues. She gives you the ability to describe thoughts and feelings based on characters' backgrounds and psychological abnormalities - about which you more than likely know nothing.

For example, how can you describe the feelings of a drug addict if you have never been one? How can you describe being in prison if you have never been to jail? Let's face it, with the internet today, you can do a huge amount of believable research, but you still have to be able to write a convincing portrayal of your characters, even if you have never lived in their skin.

Rachel to the rescue!

In *Breathing Life into Your Characters*, this professional psychotherapist shows you how to get in touch with thoughts and feelings necessary to truly understand your fictional community.

If you do not know why your characters act as they do, you do not know your characters and, sadly, neither will your readers. ~ Jessica Page Morrell

You'll learn how to develop psychological profiles and turn archetypes into conflicted characters. Remember no conflict, no story! And Rachel offers you various types of conflict, emotional flaws and fatal flaws.

Rachel will even teach you how to think like a criminal so that you can convincingly write one. This book definitely deserves another permanent place on your writing reference shelf if you're serious about building believable fictional characters.

Character Traits

By Linda Edelstein

Turning to Linda's table of contents immediately hooked my interest, with chapter 1 telling me I would learn about creating real people for my novels. Other chapters tease me with hints of how I will learn to turn my characters into real people with all manner of flaws.

This alone excites any novelist, author and aspiring writers when they are piecing together the puzzle of their new book. What makes a man have an affair? Or why a does a woman stalk her former love? What motivates these behaviours?

Linda dives straight into a writer's psyche, telling us that the huge amount of psychological research and vast vats of data is there to help writers create authentic characters. Her own experience working with people gives her insight into the interior lives of real people and what makes them happy or sad, what motivates them and what brings them to a screeching halt.

A~Z of Writers' Character Quirks

By Paula Wynne

Creating real fictional characters is one of the most important steps in writing a novel.

When you write a novel, the first thing to learn is how to create fictional characters, from heroes and heroines, to baddies and villains and other minor characters. Without a compelling character you don't have a story!

Whether they will be an animated object, toy or animal, a monster, alien or fantasy fabrication or real human beings, they need to be fully developed with emotions, flaws, hurts and habits or quirks.

But even if a writer creates an archetype character, a fictional person from a star sign, or a hero or heroine from the enneagram types, they must end up being a character with personality. You have to give them unique traits and characteristic to make them real and not a walking cardboard.

After you've started with a basic character and then added 'real flesh' to your character's bones with different personality traits and emotions, you'll need to put a lot of thought, research and time into developing a fully-fledged individual. Another way to ensure your characters are like real people is to give them habits and quirks.

One of the hardest and most satisfying parts of writing is making your characters fully alive so your readers can recognise them, visualise them, believe in them and care about them. And worry about them so much that they keep turning the pages to see what happens to the character and how they cope with the plots twists thrown at them.

Of course, this requires careful use of story events, flashbacks, memories and dialogue. Along with disorders, traits, past hurts and personality flaws, it's also helpful to flesh characters out with distinctive quirks and habits to make them memorable and distinctive.

Don't Just Create a Character ~ Create a Memorable Fictional Person

Quirks and habits serve several purposes in fiction. Inside this book I explain a few major uses for character habits and quirks, such as:

- Bringing Characters to Life with Quirks and Habits
- Identifying Characters
- Defining Character
- Creating Conflict
- Habits and Quirk Shifts

As part of the Writers' Resource Series, the *A~Z of Writers's Character Quirks* will give you a long list of Behaviours, Foibles, Habits, Mannerisms & Quirks in an easy to find alphabetical order to help you create memorable fictional characters.

Look Out For ...

Go back and tap into the book by Jeff Gerke on *Plot Versus Character* to remind yourself that your story can be driven by either the plot or the character. If you are juggling between a character who wants their story told or a plot that needs to be exploited, read Jeff's excellent book to learn the craft of writing stories that marry plot and character.

Character Viewpoint

With Deep Point of View you will give your readers such a vivid experience that they feel the events of the story are real and they're right there. ~ Rayne Hall

Characters and Viewpoint

By Orson Scott Card

Characters and Viewpoint really shone light on upping my novel's game. Orson guides you through several options to grip your readers and make them turn those pages. Suffering, sacrifice, jeopardy, tension and signs are all excellent methods to try in your written work.

Using this along with some of the points in James Scott Bell's 'ultimate revision checklist' (see the chapter on Self-Editing), I had a great time and got very excited with my rewrite. One great tip I used from James was to take certain scenes and jot down ten ideas of how to raise the stakes. Combined with Orson's value-added chapter on raising stakes, let me tell you - you can only come out with some powerful stuff!

Orson's chapter on transformations in your characters is vital to making your fictional characters real.

My favourite section of Orson's book was part three, performing characters, where he discusses voice (aka – who is telling your story) and presentation versus representation, which is about how to relate your story to your reader.

Understanding Viewpoint

If you have ever struggled with deciding if your character should speak directly to your reader, if your writing is meant to read like a real document, if you want to express an opinion or if you want to express through the point of view of a character, you seriously need to study this section!

The chapter where Orson explains dramatic versus narrative is extremely helpful for the show and tell dilemma mentioned above. And then he dives straight into chapters on first person and third person and changing viewpoints of characters.

Again, highly important things every aspiring author needs to tackle. If you have been confused with which viewpoint to use, Orson's book is a must. The knowledge he shares about viewpoint and how your reader can get deeper inside your character is essential for your story's success.

Deepening Viewpoints

For a new writer it can be mind boggling to read all the variants on how you can show your character viewpoints, but Orson makes the subject of character viewpoint easier to understand because he goes into such great detail. He even shows you how to express a character's thoughts at a deeper level of their viewpoint.

Of course, as he says, it is up to the author to make up their own mind about how they use viewpoint in their novel and how deeply to penetrate the viewpoint character's mind, but when he shows you the levels of penetration with diagrams, it helps to understand what he is teaching.

After I read this excellent book, I put it aside, played with the viewpoint ideas in my writing and then went back to read it again.

Mastering Viewpoints

Viewpoint is complex. No doubt about that, but when you digest this kind of in-depth advice, it could take some time to get to grips with it.

Deep penetration is 'hot' narration; no other story strategy keeps the reader so closely involved with the character and the story. ~ Orson Scott Card

Orson tells us that mastery of different levels of penetration is a vital part of bringing your characters to life. This is where you have the most control over your readers' experience, where you have the best chance to determine how well readers will know your characters and how much they'll care.

I highly recommend Orson's book to understand viewpoint and, more importantly, to use the techniques laid out before you by Orson.

This is by far the best book I have come across that explains all the intricate nuances of a character's viewpoint.

Taking the advice in this book, along with the simple yet practical strategies in Rayne Hall's fabulous eBook on writing a deeper point of view, you simply can't go wrong.

An intimate story takes us to a specific place and coaxes us to remain there. It feels as real and complicated as the world the reader inhabits. ~ Jessica Page Morrell

To ensure a finely polished novel, read both books. Read them in tandem or separately and then apply all the writing tools to your novel to give your readers an intimate journey with your fictional people!

Writing Deep Point of View

By Rayne Hall

Do you want to give your readers such a vivid experience that they feel the events of the story are real and they're right there?

I am sure you intend to make them forget their own world, like cooking dinner or taking the kids to ballet after school. I am equally sure you want your readers to live in the main character's head and heart. I certainly want my readers to forget their worries and be swept away with my characters.

Rayne shows new writers the magic wand for achieving this 'Deep Point of View.'

She explains that a deep point of view is a recent development. Victorian authors didn't know its power. They wrote stories from a god-like perspective, knowing everything, seeing into everyone's mind and soul. 20th century writers discovered that when they let the reader into just one person's head, stories became more exciting and real.

Living Inside Your Character's Head

By exploring this subject in greater depth with Rayne, you discover that if you take being in a character's head one step further, and delve so deeply into their mind that the reader's awareness merges with that character's, then, hey-presto, you will have a deeper point of view.

If you read extensively in the genre you are writing (and you should!), when you find this, you will love it because it gives you the thrill of becoming a different person. Your reader isn't just reading a story about a gladiator in the arena, an heiress in a Scottish castle, an explorer in the jungle, a courtesan in Renaissance Venice ~ she actually becomes that gladiator, heiress, explorer or courtesan.

In this eBook about character deep point of view, Rayne reveals many powerful techniques plied by bestselling authors. Better still, she shows you how to apply them to rivet your readers.

Places by Character Career

After the basic explanation of Point of View, Rayne teaches you about first, second and third person viewpoints and how to filter through your character's interests.

For example, a chef entering a kitchen in your novel will see the block of knives, the type of hob, the three kinds of herb vinegar, and the bunch of bananas which need to be used today because their peels have brown spots.

In contrast, your interior designer character will take in the flaking paint on the window frame, the 1980s wallpaper pattern, and the orange-coloured crockery that clashes with the pink tiles.

Likewise, if you've created an estate agent, they can't help but notice the size and layout of the room, the peeling paint on the window frames, the modern oven, the outdated sink, the extractor fan and the smoke alarm.

The point here is clear. Each character will notice these details even when they're not on the job. It's so ingrained in them to see those things, they can't help themselves. Have you used this technique for deepening your character's POV? It is well worth going back through your work to check for these finer details.

In the same way, you would create so much more atmosphere if you focus on the senses, like sounds and smells, in which your POV perceives them. This creates a more effective atmosphere than using simple visual descriptions

In one section, Rayne explains that some people have a pronounced sense of hearing, or a strong sense of rhythm. Others notice colours, or shapes, or sizes. Some are particularly aware of movement or of speed.

Yet others have finely-tuned noses and immediately notice the faintest whiff of any pleasant or unpleasant scent. And some people are particularly sensitive to temperatures, or about how textures feel to the touch.

If you use this skill in your writing, your readers are drawn right in and become that character. That's the aim, after all!

Alpha and Beta Points of View

Not many aspiring authors think about this, when writing the first draft, but men and women experience the world differently. Rayne tells you how they're programmed to notice different things. This is important for authors who write from the POV of the opposite gender.

Look at this example:

Female PoV: She scanned the contents of the trunk: an embroidered shawl, a wide-skirted gown of crimson brocade, several pieces of old lace, a velvet cloche hat, a toy car and some tools.

Male PoV: He scanned the contents of the trunk: three slotted screwdrivers, a claw hammer, combination pliers, a matchbox-sized model of a Chrysler Imperial, and some old clothes.

Immediately you see that if you are in a male head, we should see different things through the character's eyes than if you're in a female head.

Other chapters include: Situation and Mood Filters, Character Emotions and Body Language. If, like many new writers, you are struggling with character point of view, this eBook is a must have resource.

Look Out For ...

Take a look at *The Positive Trait Thesaurus* and *The Negative Trait Thesaurus* by Angela Ackerman and Becca Puglisi listed in Dictionaries and Thesauruses. They offer lots of writing tips at the end of each 'emotion' to deepen and strengthen your characters.

Character Templates

When writing a novel a writer should create living people; people not characters. A character is a caricature. ~ Ernest Hemingway

Creating Characters

By Howard Lauther

This book could easily be listed as a dictionary for its list of internal and external traits. For example, it takes vague words like 'sociable' and 'unsociable' and gives you a list of related traits with a thesaurus of different words to use to describe that trait.

The book breaks down what your character may want or need, dislike or like, fear or believe. It goes through layers of strengths and weaknesses and habits for your characters.

This is definitely a handy resource for finding out more about your story people and getting deeper inside their heads.

What is the Enneagram

If you are not into the Zodiac for creating people for your novels, try reading some of these books for another sure-fire way to ensure your goodies and baddies are multi-dimensional.

Principles of the Enneagram

By Karen Web

This diddy little book explains how the Enneagram works. The Enneagram (pronounced ~ Any-a-gram) describes nine personality types, none better or worse than the other, yet recognisably and radically different in their way of responding to the world. The book deals mainly with the psychological aspects of each Enneagram type. This is where the power of the Enneagram is able to help authors create, know and understand their characters. It is a great little book to introduce you to using Enneagram types as characters.

The Enneagram Made Easy

By Renee Baren and Elizabeth Wagele

Along with the book above, you will find this book easy for getting to grips with the Enneagram types. In fact, *The Enneagram Made Easy* is probably easier to read and get your head around the study of types of people. It explains why we behave the way we do and has sketches of each of the nine types at different events with speech bubbles so you can see their thoughts and dialogue.

For example, a drawing of 'Before the Dinner Party' shows different people looking in the mirror, and each one has something different to say. This gives you a quick snapshot of the Enneagram type's personality traits.

Each type has what they are worst at and best at, how to get along with that type, relationship points, what it is like being that type and many more topics under each type. Each of the nine types finishes with practical suggestions and exercises so you can get your bubbling pot a boost of inspiration. Then, just as Aladdin slipped out of his lamp in a puff of smoke, so too will your character appear magically to you.

This is really a must-have book for helping to make your fictional people real. When you are happy with the concept, and you have mastered what the nine types are all about, you can move into 'big boy books' like ...

The Literary Enneagram
By Judith Searle

This is the ultimate in Enneagram studies for creating exceptional fictional people. Along with a detailed chapter of how the Enneagram works and a diagram of how the different types connect with each other, *The Literary Enneagram* also provides sub-types.

Additionally, it lists how each type reacts under stress, or when they're cosy and secure. This helps you to define the high-point moments when your character is finding that the climactic stakes have turned against them. Each type has numerous literary examples showing characters in Enneagram action. This book is not for the faint-hearted.

If you are serious about learning more about how the Enneagram can create realistic personalities in your books, it is well worth having a copy that you can dip in and out of when planning and plotting your novels.

A Writer's Guide to the Zodiac
By Giselle Green

After writing my second book, *Pimp My Site*, I started rewriting one of my novels that I realized needed some work on the characters to turn them into real life people, not just names in a book.

To do this I used several great titles that provide advice for creating characters as well as information on the zodiac and stars. Although some people think it is a bunch of 'hog-wash,' the zodiac is a great guide to forming various character traits, personality flaws and foibles that we all encounter in the best fiction 'people.'

Enter ... *A Writer's Guide to the Zodiac: How the Stars Can Help You Understand Your Characters!*

For starters, the book will not frighten off the nervous or anyone vaguely doubtful of star signs and the zodiac. It is a slim 'little' offering with quick reference to each star sign. But don't be fooled by the 'slim;' it packs a big punch!

The cover is delightful, with each star sign stepping out onto the red carpet in high heels that relate to their star symbol. They're all lovely shoes, but take a look at Libra and how the 'scales' are balancing. Clever.

Astrology offers writers a powerful tool - a means by which to get to know the characters in any story - how they feel, think, and what motivates them.

As your knowledge about the individual energies associated with the star signs develops, each of your characters begins to come alive, and their destiny is revealed.

In this book, Giselle examines the zodiac in terms of the four elements: earth, fire, air and water. She describes the twelve sun signs and relates them to the elements.

Throughout the book, she shows you examples of characters from well-known books and explains how even characters with the same motivation may desire a different outcome. This is a book which makes the patterns of the zodiac accessible not only to the writer, but to anyone who has an interest in astrology.

So back to the content – the book allowed me to really climb inside the different star signs' minds to ensure that my characters are complex, humanly believable and truly three dimensional.

Lots of little … that word again … details which mean so much when forming real people in your books.

I won't spoil it for you and give you examples, you have to see them for yourself and choose which star sign will 'star' as your hero or heroine and who will be your mortal enemy!

Well done, Giselle, your book will inspire many great works of fiction and help many authors and aspiring writers to bring their characters alive.

This book is a MUST for all authors, novelists, writers, aspiring writers and self- published authors! All of these writer types ought to have a permanent copy of this little book on their reference shelf. It's very handy when creating your character, and while you're writing, it's easy to dip in and out to check that your character traits are in line.

45 Master Characters

By Victoria Lynn Schmidt

How do you start to build fictional characters when you're an aspiring writer or author?

Using Victoria Lynn Schmidt's archetypes will help you make sense of your characters and their world. It certainly will help you to address, explore and deal with current situations coming out of your plot.

Before you are put off by the word 'Archetypes' – they are, quite simply, unconscious image patterns that cross cultural boundaries.

Like Zodiac signs for building characters, archetypes form the basic skeleton of your novel's characters. But of course, you can't stop with the skeleton - unless your book is about living skeletons – and even then you'll need to add flesh and blood (figuratively speaking) and thoughts and feelings.

If you think of a stereotype for your character it only gives you a general idea – it doesn't tell you anything about their motivation, goals and fears.

Victoria's *45 Master Characters* helps you to make exciting discoveries about your book's people. Using her guidance and your plot points, you will find ways to show how your character will react to the situation (your plot).

This is what drives your story forward, not the plot point itself. A character doesn't decide to go into a burning building because that is what your plot point says he should do – he goes inside because it is in his nature to do so.

This book is an invaluable tool for all aspiring writers and novelists.

It forces you to delve deeper into your characters and see them as a types of people who respond to the conflict in your story in a very specific way.

I enthusiastically recommend that you read *45 Master Characters* and use it as a blueprint for creating your next fictional character.

Heroes & Heroines: Sixteen Master Archetypes

By Tami D Cowden, Caro LaFever and Sue Vides

This template of fictional characters starts with a list of eight Hero and Heroine archetypes. The authors give a broad analysis of the basic male and female archetypes populating the film and literature world. There are examples of several of these types as they are shown in action in books and films.

Using these archetypes to create your characters can be easily accomplished when reading this book. These 'universal character types' can be flexed and moulded into shape with your story structure and plot threads in mind.

If you are waiting for inspiration from a character, let them speak to you by reading through the list of archetypes to see if one of them springs off the page at you and begins to form into a real person in your mind.

Each type has a basic description, along with their personality qualities and virtues. Their flaws are also listed to ensure you give them layers to peel off. Remember that flaws in your characters create empathy in your reader's mind and heart, so explore the flaws and backgrounds of the different archetypes.

For every archetype, the authors have listed 'styles' which indicate what they could become. For example, the 'Chief' might be a born leader. If so, loss of control will scare him. Yet the born leader has always been aware of his destiny. Think Yul Brynner in *The King and I*. Or Al Pacino as Don Michael Corleone in *The Godfather 2*.

You will also find an extensive section on interactions between the archetypes, which contains some useful examples of how the different types can be paired to create conflict and tension.

By using the core archetypes, it becomes easy enough to turn them into your own fictional people. Little notes in the margins are also a quick and easy reference for you to find a type that suits your plot.

However, you can evolve the personality from one to another. You can also layer them. All this is shown to you in section three of the book. The authors illustrate the advantage of combining archetypes to create more complex characters.

If you are crafty enough, you can take an archetype and give him or her a horrible wound from their past that churns at them and changes them into the villain, similar to what *45 Master Characters* does in showing you the good and bad side of each personality type.

Look Out For ...

Also check out the chapter on genre writing again; it shows you how Steven Piziks' book, *Writing a Paranormal Novel*, helps you learn about supernatural fictional character growth.

Creating Villains

The best villains are complicated, unforgettable, and intensely motivated. ~ Jessica Page Morrell

Bullies, Bitches and Bastards

By Jessica Page Morrell

Create good 'Baddies' when you start building fictional characters for your novel with aggressive bullies, nasty bastards and dangerous bitches.

We know that a truly memorable antagonist is not a one-dimensional super villain bent on world domination for no particular reason.

Three-dimensional, credible bad guys create essential story complications, personalize conflict, add immediacy to a story line, and force the protagonist to evolve.

Every established author, and even aspiring writers, know they must create good baddies in order to make their novel a bestseller and have readers turning pages super fast.

Jessica explores the rise in popularity of anti-heroes, how anti-heroes possess some of the same qualities of villains but with the soul of a hero, and how these complicated characters reflect contemporary society.

From unlikable protagonists and dark heroes to bullies and mischief makers to villains and arch nemeses, *Bullies, Bastards and Bitches* shows readers how to create nuanced bad guys who are indispensable to the stories in which they appear.

A character's single most important job in a story is to stimulate the reader's emotions. Character traits should be designed to not only show them in action but, just as importantly, to show them falling apart at the seams under duress when they're involved in an extreme or highly emotional situation.

Very early in the book you'll encounter a table showing primary traits, where you list three to six traits that will showcase your character throughout the story and which will act as the foundation to their being.

A list of secondary traits is also important to support their primary traits, add depth and of course, include mannerisms and habits. Counter contrasting traits within one character, and you will expose your character's deepest layers and bring to the surface their vulnerabilities.

Sounds like you're being horrid to the 'squatters' in your head, but actually this is what really makes them believable and interesting.

Read *Bullies, Bitches and Bastards* to be sure your nasty characters are as real as your heroic story people.

The Power of the Dark Side

By Pamela Jayne Smith

Pamela's entertaining style of writing introduces aspiring authors to creating dark villains, dangerous situations and dramatic conflict.

She starts by defining the dark side, explaining what is evil and why evil can be so alluring. More importantly, she describes the difference between evil and bad and explains how we can learn from evil.

Since conflict is the heart of every story, these principles apply in any genre. Pamela states that it is vitally important for new and established authors to understand the dark side so we don't create silly stereotypes or laughable situations.

Instead, she teaches us different types of baddies and how they operate. From bad boys and girls to witches and warlocks to ghosts and ghouls, you will confront dark personalities and get into their psyches.

Essentially, Pamela will guide you through testing your baddies' weaknesses and strengths. And we all know that your villains can't be all bad! They need to be full-blown people like the other fictional characters marching around in your novels.

Writing about Villains

By Rayne Hall

Rayne bolts straight off the starting line by demanding that we forget the cardboard evil-doers with their evil laughter and stinking breath.

Our villains must have personality, ideals, feelings and conflicts. They must challenge our heroes, chill our readers, and give our novels excitement and depth.

This book in Rayne's Writing Craft series shows you how to create fiends whom readers love to hate and can't forget.

In the first chapters, Rayne taps into the power of archetypes without stereotyping to ensure we make our villains fearsome, believable and unique.

Then she explores simple yet effective sentences that will bring your fiend to life and make your reader's skin crawl.

Evil Archetypes

Certain types of characters have played a role in storytelling since humans discovered language, explains Rayne. They appear again and again, always recognisable, yet always different. They resonate with the reader's subconscious on a deep level.

The archetype is an important part of the villain's characterisation - but it's not a substitute for proper character development. Unless fleshed out as individuals, archetypes remain lifeless.

Within the pages of Rayne's excellent book, you'll find a list of the ten archetypes. If you're starting a new work of fiction, choose the one that intrigues you, and use it as the basis for the characterisation and to deepen the character.

Evil is Boring

In a chapter on evil villains, Rayne advocates that our readers will tire quickly of pure evil. Worse still, they will forget the foul villain as soon as they've finished the book. To give your story excitement and make your villain memorable, give him an objective with a well-defined goal, strong motivation and means:

- The goal is what the villain wants
- The motivation is why he wants it
- The means is how he goes about getting it

Bad Profile

Get to know your villain as well as you know your heroes, and develop a full character profile for her. This is important advice that Rayne offers to help make your book a success.

She also suggests you increase your novel's emotional impact by making the hero and the villain alike. Of course, they're very different - one is good, one is evil - but you can find and emphasise similarities. This gives the reader a deeper understanding of both, and adds an extra dimension to your story. Find a stack of ideas on how to do this and use them to deepen your baddie's profile.

A Good Baddie

When you explore the baddie's good side, you'll ensure your villains are three-dimensional and memorable. Rayne is not suggesting faked compassion or carefully planned tokens of philanthropy to impress others, but genuine goodness.

The villain can have ideals and values of which the reader approves. Create something the villain really cares about besides herself and her goal.

Rayne also shows you how to add henchmen and minions to the hero versus villain confrontation to create an unforgettable climax that your readers will be thinking about long after they've turned the final page.

The All Important Lair

Rayne supplies you with a list of equipment, furnishing and decorations for your villain's lair. She even shows you how to discover escape routes and means of communication.

Before you create your next story, start by drawing out your villain with this exciting, yet villainous eBook!

Look Out For ...

Read *45 Master Characters* for templates on how to create your villains. Each character template shows the good and bad side of the archetype character so you can bend and shape them as you please. Read the chapter on blueprints to see how to use this book with other great novel templates.

Character Emotions

It is often when emotions and actions are the most intense that you, the writer, must pull back to avoid melodrama instead of exploiting the scene. ~ Jessica Page Morrell

Emotion Thesaurus

By Angela Ackerman and Becca Puglisi

Give your characters' emotional impact with this excellent list of character emotions. Quite simply, you cannot do without this *Emotion Thesaurus* when you are creating your fictional characters!

As an aspiring novelist, you need to ensure that your reader can relate to your fictional characters. Your reader needs to feel the depth of emotion being experienced. Angela and Becca explain that, as emotional beings, feelings propel us. They drive our choices, determine who we spend time with, and dictate our values. Emotion also fuels our communication, allowing us to share meaningful information and beliefs with others.

As authors and writers, even aspiring writers, we must take our own skills in observing people around us and transfer those experiences to the page. We all know that readers have high expectations. The bestselling charts certainly seem to rub that in our 'wannabe-novelist' noses.

Your readers don't want to be told how a character feels. No, no, no. They want to experience the emotion for themselves. To make this happen, you must ensure that your fictional story people express their emotions in ways that are both recognizable and compelling to read.

Why?

Because, above all else, the reader wants to have an emotional experience with your story. They read to connect with characters who provide entertainment and whose trials may add meaning to their own life journeys.

Angela immediately makes one thing clear: dialogue is a proven vehicle for expressing a character's thoughts, beliefs, and opinions, but by itself, it cannot deliver a full emotional experience.

To convey feelings that sparkle and bounce off the page, thus making the character believable, you must also use non-verbal communication, which can be broken down into three elements:

- Physical signals (body language and actions)
- Internal sensations (visceral reactions)
- Mental responses (thoughts)

I won't spoil things by telling you what Angela says about each of these points, but she certainly makes sense. In fact, once you have grasped that each of these elements plays a vital role in breathing life into your character, believable people should start hopping about throughout your novel's pages.

When writing to portray a certain emotion, think about your body and what happens to it when you're feeling that way. The mirror will help you to note how characters may act when they're experiencing emotions and feelings. The face is the most noticeable, but the rest of the body can be just as telling. Don't overlook changes in a person's voice, speech, or overall bearing and posture.

You may want to spend time watching people—real flesh-and-blood specimens –from a park bench or coffee spot on the edge of a shopping centre. Or you can even study characters in movies. And of course, you can always pick up a copy of Angela and Becca's *Emotion Thesaurus.*

Why You Need Emotions in Your Characters

Understanding why you need emotions in your characters is a good starting point for fleshing out your characters. It is easy to see how powerful emotion can be and more importantly, how it can connect a reader to the story and characters. The difficulty comes in writing it well.

Each scene must achieve a balance between showing too little feeling and showing too much. Above all, the emotional description needs to be fresh and engaging.

Clichés in literature are vilified for good reason. They're a sign of lazy writing, and all too often writers will fall back on clichés.

Write the emotion well, develop empathy in your reader, maximize the words that you do use, but don't overstay your welcome.

This is a tall order for writers who tend to reuse the same emotional indicators over and over.

Angela and Becca give a sterling example of just how you can look right into the character and know so much about them from simple things like clutching their handbag with photos of their kids inside to jumping up so fast the chair skitters across the tiles.

Each emotion has a definition, along with physical signals such as touching ones face when 'adoring' someone and internal sensations like a dry mouth. It also gives mental responses for the emotion, like fixating one's thoughts on the subject - as in the emotion adoration.

Cues also help aspiring novelists to put more meat on their fictional people's bones. For example, if your character has 'adored' another, they may be obsessed, or fantasize about them or even start stalking them. That certainly gives you inspiration for creating character plot points!

And the cues show what the emotion may escalate to; for example, in the adoration scenario, frustration or even hatred may develop if the adoration goes unreciprocated. Angela gives cues for suppressed emotions, which is a better way of showing emotion than telling.

To top it off, each emotion has a writer's tip. I'll tease you with one:

To add another layer to an emotional experience, look for symbolism within the character's current setting. What unique object within the location can the character make note of that perfectly embodies the emotion they are feeling inside?

The Emotion Thesaurus helps writers brainstorm new ideas for expressing a character's emotional state. But what about other pitfalls associated with portraying emotion? This detailed thesaurus explores a few of these common trouble spots and suggests techniques for overcoming them.

I, for one, can't wait to now get caught up in my next novel and start picking out these finer points in my character's emotions. I'm also keen to find any place where monologues may scream for verbal interaction based on Angela's fine examples. I will be looking at my scene checklist, because I now realise – with the help of *Emotion Thesaurus* - emotion is much more effectively conveyed through a mixture of dialogue, thoughts, and body language. I will remember Angela's top tip...

> *When expressing emotion, vary your vehicles, using both verbal and non-verbal techniques for maximum impact.* ~ Angela Ackerman

After reading 'Making Faces,' I realised a good item for a writer's or author's home office is a mirror. Sounds odd, doesn't it? But it makes sense if you're writing about a character and, in particular, their emotions and body language that you could 'practise' in front of the mirror.

When writing, I often find myself balancing precariously on my chair, bobbing up and down or slanting side to side as I try to re-enact what my character is doing. So why not look in the mirror to see what kind of emotions your character is expressing?

Angela says, 'I think emotion should be added in stages. Before a writer begins drafting they should know their characters well enough to understand how their individual personality will affect emotional responses.'

If a main character is introverted, shy or secretive, likely he or she would express emotion much differently than a person who is outgoing, confident, or even eccentric. Understanding a bit of the character's backstory will help form who they are, which in turn will allow the writer to draft realistic emotional displays that align with their personality.

Then during later drafts, emotions can be deepened to become more meaningful, tuning in to the story's theme.

Read *Emotion Thesaurus* now! I highly recommend it for showing and not telling and for engaging your readers with deeper layers of characterisation.

Emotional Impact

By Karl Iglesias

Like Jessica Page Morrell's *Between the Lines*, it was difficult to decide where to put Karl's book. Although titled 'Writing for Emotional Impact' this book is not about character emotions alone.

In fact, it is about the whole emotional experience you feel as the writer of your fiction. And equally, the emotional experience your reader will feel when reading your novel. Provided, of course, that you have used the techniques handed out in this and other books I have listed in *Pimp My Fiction*.

You'll see what I mean when you open the table of contents and spy chapters ranging from your reader as an audience, concept as a unique attraction, theme's universal meaning, captivating empathy in your characters, rising tension in your story, engaging design in your structure, mesmerising moments in your scenes, riveting styles in your descriptions, vivid voices with dialogue and painting pictures on your page.

Phew! See what I mean? I could have inserted Karl's book in any of the chapters because he covers it all. Essentially, Karl wants writers to view their manuscript or screenplay as the promise of an intense and satisfying emotional experience.

Word Connections

Karl believes we have to shift our thinking. Reading is a personal activity between the reader and the page, one individual connecting with words. He says a reader will only experience emotions from your words and how you string them together on the page. You're the only person responsible for the reader's emotional response. If he's bored instead of captivated, that's it. Game over.

As an aspiring writer, you need to hone your craft. But what does that mean? asks Karl. He explains that craft is knowing how to make things happen on the page.

Specifically, it's the technical ability to control language to create an intentional emotion or image in the reader's mind, hold his attention, and reward him with a moving experience. In short, craft is about connecting with the reader through words on the page. A good story well told means evoking emotion.

Great writers are in charge of the reader's emotions at all times, on every single page. That's craft. ~ Karl Iglesias

In your job to seduce your readers and make them turn your pages to see what happens next, you have to find the most exciting and emotionally involving way to tell your story. Well, Karl is just about to tell you exactly how to do that.

Intensify the Page Connection

Starting with three types of storytelling emotions and then explaining the difference between character emotions and reader emotions, Karl offers you a compass of storytelling techniques that will intensify your reader's connection to the page.

As Karl says, his advice won't automatically turn you into a great writer (nor will any of the other advice in *Pimp My Fiction*). You still need to apply the ideas to your original concepts and keep writing to hone your craft.

Karl wants all writers to start thinking: 'I'm in the emotional-delivery business, and my job is to evoke emotion in a reader.' He goes as far as to tell you to write this in big, bold letters and stick it above your work station to remind you of your duties as a writer.

New, Fresh, Compelling Concepts

A concept that is unique and fresh is always enticing. We all know that and want that for our books. And we all hear in the writing world that we should write what we know.

Karl stones that theory by telling us, don't write what you know. The best way to create something exciting is to write about what excites you, what intrigues you and what fascinates you. Sounds tough, hey? Not to worry, Karl gives you twelve ways to increase your idea's appeal.

He then goes on to give you nine theme tips to show and not tell. I'll cheat and give you a little taste here. Karl's first tip is to turn theme into a question instead of a premise. For example, rather than stating the premise for *Romeo and Juliet* as 'Great love defies even death,' you could ask, 'How powerful is a great love?' So ask a question and let your story provide us with the answer by experiencing it emotionally.

Reveal Your Character on the Page

As writers, we all want our characters to create empathy. Karl shows you in various steps how to do this when creating your characters, using their needs and motivations, goals and desires, and high stakes entwined with their character arc.

He also reveals six ways to reveal your character on the page. Spoiler alert here: in a couple of short but meaningful sentences, we can deliver a clear image of a character's appearance, personality and inner-conflict.

Karl advocates: The craft is connecting with characters. In action. On our pages.

There it is again, that word: Craft.

Each and every chapter in this valuable writing guide shunts out trolley loads of advice that you can use in every aspect of writing your novel. Look back for a moment at the subjects covered in the content of the book to imagine how much you will learn from this experienced and acclaimed author.

It's about verb-driven, visual and active sentences that move. ~ Karl Iglesias

With powerful advice for writers on every page, this is definitely one of the most beneficial books for overall guidance on creating the best work of fiction you can write. A book you should not be without when creating your next novel!

Do yourself a huge favour and start reading the whole book, cover to jam-packed cover.

Look Out For ...

More advice on showing character emotions in dialogue can be found in Gloria Kempton's book called *Dialogue*, which is featured in the chapter on writing dialogue.

Also see *Plot and Structure* by James Scott Bell, who explains how an emotional scene has something fresh and surprising and emotionally intense. It has characters we care about doing things that compel us to watch or read about.

I am currently reading *Writing the Heart of Your Story* by CS Lakin and will update you on this book in the next version, be sure you're on the Scenes Checklist download list to get your free copy.

Writing Dialogue

If you can tell stories, create characters, devise incidents, and have sincerity and passion, it doesn't matter a damn how you write. ~ Somerset Maugham

Dialogue

By Gloria Kempton

In Gloria's writing reference guide on writing dialogue, she tells you that dialogue is an accelerator. The faster you get your fictional people talking, the faster the scene moves. Cutting out any unnecessary narrative or action sentences will speed up your story. And she advises that you cut out any speech tags so that your dialogue is at bare bones.

When creating dialogue for your characters, Gloria explains that it's all in the details. Whether you're writing dialogue, action or narrative [which makes up most of your story], vivid details are what causes a reader to be able to see, hear, touch, taste and smell – in other words to be able to experience your story on a sensory level. All of these senses must come directly from the character's point of view so that the reader gets to know this fictional person on a deeper level.

Use Dialogue for Pace

Gloria tells you to only use details that enhance the mood you are trying to create and get across the emotion the character is feeling to move the plot forward. The fewer the details, the more each will stand out, and the pace will quicken. Too much of anything will slow down the pace of your story.

This writing guide explains that describing a setting can be done through your characters' eyes and thoughts. Moving this fictional person into action and throwing in setting details as the characters are chasing each other and interacting is the better way to use description.

She recommends that novelists never use narrative to describe a setting when you can have a viewpoint character describing the setting in a lively discussion with another fictional person. Description in action beats static description!

Inject Emotion into Dialogue for Impact

Most importantly, the more emotion you put into a scene the faster it moves because it heightens the tension and conflict. Characters expressing emotion are predictable and often out of control. Anything can happen, so it raises the stakes.

To quicken the pace, you can also use short sentences of dialogue with lots of white space on the page. If your characters shoot short phrases of dialogue back and forth at a rapid pace, your reader will be turning the pages.

According to Gloria, it doesn't matter if the fictional character screams or whispers, what does matter is whether the emotion is fear, sadness, joy, or anger. This makes them emotionally engaged with the situations and conflicts in the story, and they should naturally convey their feelings to one another through dialogue that is charged with emotion. The more emotion, the better!

Heighten Tension with Dialogue

Fear creates tension, not just for the characters, but for everyone around them. Thriller writers must become masters of revealing this emotion in their characters because their readers are looking for it. The emotion of fear speeds everything up and makes it all stand still at the same time, making the danger almost palpable to the reader.

If you want to be the kind of writer willing to make every scene of dialogue tense and full of suspense, then you must be willing to throw your fictional people into conflict after conflict. After all, that is what successful bestselling stories are all about.

Find out more about Gloria's book on writing dialogue.

Look Out For ...

Also check out the chapter on genre writing where you'll learn how to write good dialogue for your supernatural people in *Writing a Paranormal Novel* by Steven Piziks.

Cinematic Settings

*There's always room for a story that can transport people to
another place. ~ J.K. Rowling*

Wouldn't it be wonderful if a reader told you that your settings were
so vivid that they pictured the character in their mind like a movie screen?

I was thrilled to hear some of my beta readers say this after they read
the final draft of *The Grotto's Secret*. I was especially interested to hear
their remarks about my medieval settings because of course it is hard to
imagine living in those times.

I never studied history, but have always loved historical novels and
wanted to emulate the best historical novelists. So when I heard that my
medieval scenes were so alive to my readers, so much that they could see
them unfolding before their eyes, I was in heaven, to say the least!

These are the books that helped me to do this ...

Writing Vivid Settings

By Rayne Hall

Do you want your readers to feel as if they are right there in the place where your story is unfolding? By creating vivid settings that bring your story locations to life, your readers will breathe the cool mountain air, feel the icy wind sting their cheeks, and sink their toes into the moist sand.

Like her other eBooks on the craft of writing, Rayne arms you with powerful techniques for immersing readers in your story.

For example, Rayne explains how to use the sense of smell. She says that of all the senses, smell has the strongest psychological effect. The mere mention of a smell evokes memories and triggers associations in the reader's subconscious.

Mention a smell, and the scene comes to life. Mention two or three, and the reader is pulled into the scene as if it were real. You have probably experienced this many times when reading novels by your favourite authors. Like Rayne demonstrates to aspiring new authors, those authors have used their characters' senses to draw you into their story and keep you there.

Rayne shows how a single sentence about smells can reveal more about a place than several paragraphs of visual descriptions. This is useful if you aim to keep your descriptions short.

Rayne gives you lots of examples to try, along with how and where to use this technique. She also shows professional examples used in fiction so you can see her advice in action.

Sounds to Add Excitement

A whole chapter is dedicated to showing you how a sentence describing noises creates a strong atmosphere. And at the same time, it rouses the reader's level of excitement. Rayne goes into detail about two types of sounds: background noises and action noises.

She explains that background noises are sounds that are unrelated to the action, but add character to the places you use in your novel, so they are perfect for creating atmosphere.

With action sounds, Rayne explains that whenever characters do something, such as walk, work, fight or rest, they do it in a specific space, and their actions interact with their environment. This creates a link between the action and the setting. Emphasise this link, especially if you want the reader to become immersed in the story. The best way to do this is by describing the sounds arising from the characters' interaction with the environment.

Mood, Light and Weather Enhancers

Along with light to convey the atmosphere of a place, and using creative phrases to convey a mood, you can evoke any kind of atmosphere you want, from creepy, gritty, depressed or aggressive to romantic, optimistic and gentle.

Along with the tips and techniques she provides for ensuring your settings are vivid and real in your reader's mind, Rayne follows through with how weather can give your locations intensity.

As with all the chapters in this exciting eBook, you will be shown how and where to use the techniques, along with fictional examples and mistakes to avoid.

Other topics include:

- Detail for Realism
- Similes for World Building
- Deep POV

- Opening Scenes, Climax Scenes and Action Scenes
- Researching and Writing about Real Places

After soaking up all the techniques I found in this Craft of Writing eBook I was eager to dive right into my novel to add the new details I had just learnt.

One of my favourite chapters is 'Symbols for the Literary Touch.' After I had read this chapter, I immediately noticed that I had used a certain setting theme in *The Grotto's Secret* without even realising it. So I went back to ensure that I had applied all the tips Rayne offered on using symbols in the places your character visits.

Another easy to read and apply writing resource from an accomplished author!

Description and Setting

By Ron Rozelle

For a story to be successful, it must come alive on the page. With Description & Setting, writers will learn how to make every detail count as they create believable people, places and events.

How do you do this? By creating a believable world, which includes places where your fictional characters wander around. But just how important is setting to your story? How much description is too much? And in what ways can you, as an aspiring novelist, use setting and description to add depth to your story?

Write Great Fiction

In the *Write Great Fiction* series of writing books to improve your craft of writing, *Description and Setting* by Ron Rozelle provides practical exercises at the end of each chapter.

But as a novelist plotting out your first book, you need tips and techniques to guide you through hooking your readers with some description of the settings in which you place your fictional characters. Right?

> *Don't hide behind vagueness. Be specific, be sure, be powerful.*
> *It's the only way to write. ~ Jessica Page Morrell*

Ron intends to help you establish a realistic sense of time and place and use evocative descriptions to drive your story forward. More importantly, he aims to help you avoid the problem of having too much description cluttering your story.

In the books I have reviewed on writing a thriller (coming up), one the important points I have gleaned is to ensure you don't let description run over pages and pages, or even one page. If you want a fast-paced novel or thriller that keeps your readers moving like mad through your pages, you cannot have loads of description. Quite simply, it will slow your page right down.

So, how do you ensure that you create evocative and authentic descriptive scenes without churning your story to a halt?

Create Writing Pictures

My favourite part of Ron's book on description and setting is how to show resemblance when writing about a place for your fictional characters to be in your story with Metaphors, Similes, Analogies, Allusions and Personification.

Personification is a figure of speech that bestows human actions or sensibilities onto inanimate objects and ideas.

Ron says the use of personification is the perfect opportunity for you to make clear in your reader's mind an action that is important in your story. Saying that the warm water of a swimming hole touched a character's arm is a pretty dull description, yet notice how much more effective it is to say that the water caressed it. We have all been hit by a wave or kissed by the wind or heard the wind singing in the trees or maybe had that last piece of pie calling out our name.

Your settings mustn't be backdrops that thump down onto the stage when a scene changes. Instead, says Ron, make them vibrant and believable places.

Ron is another expert who also goes into great detail about using the five senses to bring setting and scenes to life. He gives this example of a great description from Cormac McCarthy's *Cities of the Plain*:

> *Billy peered out at the high desert. The bellied light wires raced against the night.*

Clearly this uses unexpected images – uncommon phrases – to paint precise images in the reader's mind.

Describing something or someone in such an unusual way – like McCarthy calling the power lines 'bellied' – makes the reader pay a little closer attention and remember the image better. You can just imagine the power lines having races against the desert – see how cleverly this object becomes animated.

Ron says that, as an aspiring novelist, you must pay special attention to what everything looks like, so that you can show it in your writing. You must focus on the fine points of colours, lighting, shadows, shapes and textures as closely as you note the bigger aspects of what will end up in your story pages.

In *Description and Setting*, Ron also gives you a few nuggets of writing advice. Ron suggests that whenever you do use a colon, you're setting up your reader for something:

1. A description
2. A clarification
3. An idea
4. A list

Ron believes it's one of the best ways for you to call attention to something important in your story. I'm going to give that a go and see if that improves my writing style.

Foreshadowing in Your Novel

Besides showing new writers how to use descriptions in their settings, Ron tells novelists that foreshadowing gives the reader a clue – a taste of what is to come – like a formation of geese ahead of an approaching cold front.

Listen to the first sentence Ron gives us about foreshadowing a novel, from Alice Sebold's *The Lovely Bones*:

My name was Salmon, like the fish; first name, Susie.

In this example Ron explains that the word packed with foreshadowing is the verb 'was'. Why? Most readers will want to know, isn't her name still Susie Salmon? Why is she using past tense? The very next sentence answers that:

I was murdered on December 6, 1973.

Now readers want to know how and why she was murdered… and what the heck is going on here.

101 Writers' Scene Settings

By Paula Wynne

Scene Settings are critical pieces of the puzzle that will eventually make up your entire novel.

It might be new settings that you require or maybe vamping up current scene locations that are not fitting snugly into the rest of your plot.

Most of the time writers and authors use scene settings that we know and thus naturally come with a sense of comfort. But what about exciting our readers with new places for them to experience through your characters? After all, the reason readers read is to travel to new places, meet new people and experience new emotions ~ all through your stories.

As writers we are taught that everything in our scenes must be seen through the eyes of our PoV characters. This is vitally important when looking at the scene settings. Your hero may love a certain place, but someone else, possibly your villain, will hate it. The same will happen when you browse through the list of settings ideas. More importantly, 101 Writer's Scene Settings is aimed at generating deeper opinions from you if that particular setting may work for your story, or if it inspires something else in you.

Don't Just Write A Scene ~ Write A Memorable Setting

Make your scene settings come alive to your readers with mood, senses, atmosphere and vivid descriptions shown through the point of view of your characters. This book will guide you through choosing settings with mood, atmosphere and sensory details that will influence your characters.

In films like Bourne or Bond you see baddies chasing the hero through crowded towns with tight corners and narrow streets or racing across roof tops. In other classic films you may see the most unusual places on earth and wonder how the studios found those places to feature in their films. Clearly they have endless budgets with numerous bodies to scout for locations. But what if there was a resource where writers could dip in and out to find these special types of locations for setting their scenes?

101 Writers' Scene Settings will guide you through:

- Finding unique locations for different scenarios in your plot
- Creating vivid descriptions for your scene setting and weaving them together seamlessly through the character's actions and reactions
- Develop all the elements within a location to ensure you write realistic, intriguing descriptions shown from the character's point of view
- Using sensory details that bring your setting to life
- Layers of details that make a reader feel like they are right there with your character
- And you will get a free download copy of the Settings Checklist!

Filled with ideas for categories such as crowded towns, tight and narrow streets, adventure locations, places up high and down below, mountains and valleys, seascapes, abandoned places, modern techno, scary and spooky, and unusual work places, homes and fight scenes, 101 *Writers' Scene Settings* helps you to dive into researching and planning your settings so you can write a compelling scene that readers won't forget.

Includes advice from successful authors: Linda Abbott, Steve Alcorn, James Becker, Glenn Cooper, Jeff Gerke, Angela Marsons, CS Lakin, Marti Leimbach, Rayne Hall, Alex Myers, Jodie Renner, Douglas E. Richards, Joyce Schneider.

Look Out For ...

Also check Gloria Kempton's advice in my listing under 'Dialogue,' where she shows how you can describe locations through dialogue.

Another good resource, which I mentioned earlier, is *Writing the Picture* by Robin U Russin and William Missouri Downs who show how to use picture-making words that help to make your scenes come alive.

I am also reading *Shoot Your Novel* by CS Lakin and will update you on this book in the next version, be sure you're on the Scenes Checklist download list to get your free copy.

Sci-Fi, Supernatural and Fantasy

I like nonsense, it wakes up the brain cells. Fantasy is a necessary ingredient in living; it's a way of looking at life through the wrong end of a telescope. Which is what I do, and that enables you to laugh at life's realities. ~ Dr. Seuss

Writing about Magic

By Rayne Hall

Are you writing about magic or magicians or witches or anything to do with Fantasy Fiction?

After Rayne Hall showed us how to put the eeeek into writing scary scenes for those of us writing thrillers (see the chapter on writing a thriller), I thought it apt that she weave a little bit of magic over us to get us into the mood for those of you writing fantasy.

Rayne's eBook, *Writing about Magic*, starts off by explaining the personality and profile of Magician characters. If your novel's heroine or the hero or the evil villain have any magical qualities, and you have any magical minor characters - such as a witch, a ritual wizard, a theurgist, an alchemist, a shaman – then you can use this eBook to deepen the characterisation of your magical people.

Creating Your Magician

Certain personality traits are common among magicians, and certain talents help them with their craft, so it's helpful that Rayne guides us through suggestions for characterisation. Your magician should have most - not necessarily all - of these character traits. For example, one personality trait would be Intelligence. After all, magic requires a sharp intellect, critical thinking, critical analysis and the ability to make difficult decisions!

Choosing a Magic System

Rayne goes on to explain how you can choose a magic system, be it high magic or low magic, black and white magic, ceremonial or natural magic or even witchcraft. You invent your magic system with terms and definitions (helped along with advice from Rayne's magic experience) and you create spells to cast on your characters.

Beware, though; there are many blunders a new writer of fantasy should avoid. Thankfully Rayne gives us a list of blunders – as she does in each chapter under each magical theme. Phew!

Along with the training and initiation of your magician, you'll need to consider what rituals, locations and circle casting your story will include. You can't just suck this stuff out of your thumb. Rayne certainly shows us self-published writers that there are some power-raising spells to be cast over our own novels before we can self-publish.

There are charts and the costumes and equipment your plot will need. And you may need to learn what writing strategies to follow if your plot involves love spells or sex magic! You'll really need to get your grubby paws on this eBook to find out about that topic.

Fiction isn't written to make readers happy. Its purpose is to jangle their nerves, make their hearts race, give them goosebumps and disturb their sleep. ~ Jessica Page Morrell

Magical Weapons and Warfare

Then Rayne delves into magical weapons and warfare and goes into much detail about the materials you can use when you create your magic weapons. You need to consider their shape and size, how they work, and the discharging and cleaning of the weapons. What I really like about this eBook on writing magic is that Rayne gives you plot possibilities for all scenarios. Having someone explain how to create magical weapons is one thing, but having them also give you plot ideas is highly useful for the new writer of fantasy.

Of course, healing and protection goes with magical warfare, so soon after finding out how to create your novel's weapons you'll be learning how to guard your characters against curses and harmful magic.

Conflicts and Secrets in Magic

Before Rayne finishes her eBook about writing magic, she explains ethics, conflicts and secrecy and how a Mage could make mistakes – along with plot suggestions as usual. She closes on magic in the future and gives you lots of food for thought to weave magic into your own self-published novels.

A Brief Guide to the Supernatural

Dr Leo Ruickbie

A Brief Guide to the Supernatural: Ghosts, Vampires and the Paranormal by Dr Leo Ruickbie is a writing resource for those writers who are new to supernatural elements in a novel. If you intend to self-publish your novel, it will need to be well-researched and up to date on what writing about the supernatural really means.

However, writers who are old hats at writing supernatural stories can also learn from this documented guide in all the major areas of the paranormal.

Ghosts to Vampires

From 'Most Haunted' to 'Buffy the Vampire Slayer,' from 'Underworld' to 'Twilight,' from 'Doom' to 'Resident Evil,' this guide goes in search of everything and anything that is unearthly. Leo expertly combines history, science, psychology and myth and explores the allure of the paranormal, as well as the many ways people have tried to contact and record the impossible.

In your research for your own supernatural novel, you will need to find out how humans experience different phenomena and entity contacts, and how we have attempted to understand and explain them.

In this book on the Supernatural you'll find that Dr Leo has carved out a guide that will be immensely useful to writers of the paranormal.

Leo's writing guide can be classed as a glossary of facts, figures and fictions. *A Brief Guide to the Supernatural* can be used as an introduction to the world of all things ghoulish and eerie and scary and out of this world. Or you can use it to dip in and out of when you need to remind yourself about spirits, angels and demons.

If you're the spooky writer amongst us, this guide needs to be on your bookshelf!

The Enclyclopedia of Ghosts and Spirits

By Rosemary Ellen Guiley

This book (the size of a brick), is the second edition of this guide and it's set out almost like a dictionary. In alphabetical order, it lists everything and anything to do with spirits, ghosts and the paranormal.

This is another ideal resource to dip in and out of when writing a supernatural story that entails anything to do with ghosts, angels or demons or anything weird and magical.

It really should be listed in the dictionaries section, but it fitted so snugly here amongst the paranormal ...

Writing the Paranormal Novel
By Steven Piziks

Vampires, werewolves, and zombies, oh my!

Writing a paranormal novel takes more than casting an alluring vampire or arming your hero with a magic wand. It takes an original idea, believable characters, a compelling plot, and surprising twists, not to mention great writing.

Writing the Paranormal Novel is a helpful guide that gives you everything you need to successfully introduce supernatural elements into any story without shattering the believability of your fictional world or falling victim to common clichés.

You'll learn how to:
- Choose supernatural elements and decide what impact the supernatural will have on your fictional world
- Create engaging characters, from supernatural protagonists and antagonists to supporting players (both human and non-human)
- Develop strong plots and complementary subplots
- Write believable fight scenes and flashbacks
- Create realistic dialogue

Steven not only offers 'supernatural' advice to help you write your paranormal novel, but he gives you lots of examples of successful authors of werewolves, vampires, ghosts and wizards. These examples are good to know so that you can reach out and dig deeper into your genre to identify what you need to do as a self-published author of the same genre.

Steven's paranormal guide is written clearly, with relevant content in the selection of chapters on the subject and loads of advice stuffed between the covers. When you're reading this book, you will even learn more about fictional character growth alongside how to write good dialogue for your supernatural people.

This is a great guide for anyone delving into the world of writing supernatural or paranormal novels.

How to Write Science Fiction and Fantasy
By Orson Scott Card

If you're on a journey learning to write about fantasy, then Orson Scott Card's book called *How to Write Science Fiction and Fantasy* will provide exactly the advice you need.

If you're a self-published writer interested in constructing stories about people, worlds and events that stretch the boundaries of the possible and the magical, Orson's guide also includes information on potential markets and how to reach them.

Let's face it; you can't go wrong getting advice from one of the biggest names in science fiction and fantasy. Orson Scott Card won both the Hugo and Nebula science fiction awards for best novel for two consecutive years - something no other writer has done. In addition, he was the first writer to ever win a Nebula and a Hugo for both a book and its sequel.

If you're keen on only one of these genres you may find that not all chapters will be useful. However, you may find them interesting enough to feed your writing mind with ideas. First up, Orson answers the questions: what is science fiction and what is fantasy?

He also gives any writer picking up his book lots of meaty topics on story construction and writing well. The MICE quotient (milieu, idea, character and event) and knowing which is most important in your story will help you decide your novel's shape.

Orson arms you with a creative route into writing fantasy and science fiction and to free your imagination to run wild into building your own fantasy or science fiction worlds. *How to Write Science Fiction and Fantasy* will help you to keep your fantasy or science fiction story balanced within your new imaginary world and ensure that your characters hook your readers.

This is another excellent resource book for writers from Writers' Digest Books that you can dip in and out of at any time in your writing – be it fantasy or science fiction.

The Guide to Writing Fantasy and Science Fiction

By Philip Athans

The *Guide to Writing Fantasy and Science Fiction: 6 Steps to Writing and Publishing Your Bestseller* helps writers learn how to craft their own breakout fantasy or sci-fi novel.

This guide also helps in developing the best plot structure; creating believable, exciting characters; writing compelling combat scenes; presenting technology that sounds as if it ought to work; and finally, writing a strong proposal and finding the right publisher.

Like Orson Scott Card, who is an expert on writing fantasy and science fiction, Philip Athans is a highly qualified authority on the subject. He is managing editor of novels at Wizards of the Coast, the largest producer of fantasy hobby games in the world. He's worked with

R.A. Salvatore, as well as Margaret Weis and Tracy Hickman, creators of the bestselling Dragonlance series.

Philip has also published his own fantasy novels, including the *New York Times* bestsellers *Annihilation, the Watercourse Trilogy,* and *In Fluid Silence,* as well as *A Reader's Guide to R.A. Salvatore's The Legend of Drizzt.*

So with all that knowledge, he punches above his weight in teaching new authors how to write fantasy and science fiction.

What Are Fantasy and Science Fiction?

Philip starts the book by explaining what is fantasy and what is science fiction, and how to know your audience.

Once you have that sorted, you motor onto other interesting subjects such as storytelling, where you'll learn how to get started with an idea, developing your plot, knowing when to stop and how to write fantasy and science fiction well.

Writing Fictional Fantasy Characters

Next up is finding out how to create fictional characters for your fantasy or science fiction novel. Here Philip tells all aspiring authors of this genre to ask and answer questions, and he gives you lists of questions you should ask yourself about your fantasy people that will populate your self-published novel.

He'll guide you into writing good villains and give you tips on how to nurture your heroes. Then you'll learn how to assemble a cast of supporting characters and give them each their own voice.

It is not an easy ride, let me tell you!

You'll need to learn how to build your new fantasy world, then you have to add fictional people and concoct your magic spells.

Fantasy is my favorite genre for reading and writing. We have more options than anyone else, and the best props and special effects. That means if you want to write a fantasy story with Norse gods, sentient robots, and telepathic dinosaurs, you can do just that. Want to throw in a vampire and a lesbian unicorn while you're at it? Go ahead. ~ Patrick Rothfuss

You also need to invent fantastical names (I had fun with this by Googling for fantasy name finders), and then you have to establish a fantasy or science fiction culture and make it authentic with a history of how, when, who, why and what.

Building Your Fantasy World

Step three in Philip's six steps to writing and publishing your bestseller, is creating your world. This section covers deciding on your setting, building your world and its geography and filling this new world with monsters and people and their leaders.

Step four goes even deeper into the details of your fantasy or science fiction novel, by suggesting you try such techniques as defining a system of weights and measures. Who would have thought you'd need to do that! What language will your world use? And will there be magic and technology?

Now Philip starts getting to the 'Nuts and Bolts' of your world in step five's chapters on romance, action and humour. In the final step (six) Philip advises new authors to this genre to keep it fresh but also to follow their own rules.

More Fantasy Fiction Advice

You may want to browse through other books we have on the subject from Writers' Digest Books. Having a few books on the subject will guide you into this exciting genre, so browse through our Writing Fantasy Fiction section.

The Writer's Complete Fantasy Reference

By Writer's Digest Books

The Writer's Complete Fantasy Reference contains articles by a collection of editors and writers at Writers' Digest Books; this is an indispensable compendium of Myth and Magic for new authors delving into writing about fantasy.

For example, do you know what a murder hole is? Or why a chimera is three times worse than most monsters? And what would be better for storming castles, a trebuchet or a kopesh?

To find the answers to these questions, you need this fascinating guide to transport yourself to fantasy's mysterious worlds. If you're new to writing fantasy stories for children or even adults, you'll learn all the facts on how to write fantasy.

This genre is very popular, yet so complicated. Before authors can self-publish their fantasy novels, they need to learn how to make their fantasy fiction vibrant, captivating and original.

How to Create a Fantasy Novel

From classic medieval witchcraft to ancient Mesoamerican civilizations, every chapter in *The Writer's Complete Fantasy Reference* will spark your creativity. This invaluable resource will also help you fill your writing with inventive new ideas rooted in accurate descriptions of the world's most intriguing legends, folklore and mysticism.

If, like me, you are intending to venture into the fantastic to create magical realms alive with detail, this book will be a great basis to start your fantasy reference search.

How to Build a Fantasy World

As a writer new to the fantasy genre and researching certain elements for your fantasy novel, or even just looking for inspiration, this book is an amazing resource for you to build a fantastical new world and culture. In your new fantasy world, you'll need to decide on politics and commerce and warfare. You'll need to decide what fantasy races you'll feature – will they be Elves or Dwarves or Merfolk or Trolls; and you can choose from a band of others.

Or you can get stimulated to create a new creature from a list of creatures from Myth and Legend.

Maybe you are planning to create romps and escapes in a castle. No fear. This writing reference guide will help you with Arms, Armour and Armies as well as the anatomy of a castle.

On another note, Patricia C. Wrede offers Fantasy Worldbuilding Questions for authors of fantasy fiction who are seeking to create believable imaginary settings for their stories. You may also find her web link handy when building your world, simply by provoking your mind to start thinking about the settings and backgrounds: http://bit.ly/1iKT1Is

This site gives you a glossary of Fantasy Fiction terms that you may find useful: http://thewritingcafe.tumblr.com/post/57879584935/basics-genres-alternate-world-a-setting-that

How to Write About Magic

If you're into writing about magic, you should cast your own spell upon your family to keep them away from your door while you ponder on the sections on magic, witchcraft and fantasy races. You can find out how to recognise a witch, the difference between Traditional Witchcraft and Gothic Witchcraft, Neo-Pagan Witchcraft and New Age Neo-Pagans. Not only will you learn the language of Witchcraft and a long list of terms, but even more exciting, you'll be armed with lots of spice to add to your fantasy novel.

Being new to writing fantasy, I found *The Writer's Complete Fantasy Reference* to be a valuable source of information and ideas. Why not pop over and get your copy now.

Look Out For ...

If you're writing about time travel you may want to check the *The Time Travellers Almanac*, which is a collection of time travel stories by Ann and Jeff VanderMeer.

The anthology covers millions of years of Earth's history - from the age of the dinosaurs to strange and fascinating futures, even to the end of Time itself.

Another book I'm reading is *Creating Imaginary Worlds* by Charles Christian and will update you on this book in the next version, be sure you're on the Scenes Checklist download list to get your free copy.

Other Genres

*The novel is not so much a literary genre, but a literary space,
like a sea that is filled by many rivers. ~ Jose Saramago*

Writing Your 50 Shades Novel

IIf you're aiming to write the next *50 Shades of Grey*, here are some
sneaky books that will help you on your journey.

1001 Sexcapades to Do If You Dare

By Bobbie Dempsey

Bobbie says that an exciting sex life isn't just for Playboys or
Playboy bunnies any more. With this book on your night stand, you

will be challenged to throw away your inhibitions, increase your pleasure, and keep boredom out of your bedroom for good! There's plenty to keep the passion alive with new positions, new locations, and new twists on old favourites.

You will be tempted to try all sorts of new sexual manoeuvres and put yourself in different kinds of erotic situations with dares like: have an "Everything But..." fashion show/sex romp series; host your own hot movie festival; have a (voluntary) dry spell; practice yoga together ... in the nude; slip a pair of your panties, his favourites, into his pocket before he leaves for work; and more!

Know your literary tradition, savour it, steal from it, but when you sit down to write, forget about worshipping greatness and fetishizing masterpieces. ~ Allegra Goodman

Looking for a more adventurous session in the sack? Then try this book—if you dare.

This racy little romp of a book is said to take your love life from humdrum to hot so why can't it spice up your erotica novel?

You'll be on the road to *50 Shades of Grey fame ...*

Why Men Love Bitches

By Sherry Argov

If you're too nice, run out and get this *Why Men Love Bitches* because Sherry delivers a unique, real-life and hilarious perspective, explaining why men are attracted to a strong woman who stands up for herself.

With saucy details on every page, this no-nonsense guide reveals why a strong woman is much more desirable than a 'yes woman' who routinely sacrifices herself. The author provides answers to the tough questions women often ask.

Sherry says ... go from doormat to dream girl with this woman's guide to holding her own in a relationship.

Sexploits –an Erotic Journal
By Adams Media

You may want to delve into this sexy, fun, kinky, racy, daring little journal called *Sexploits - an Erotic Journal -* and make notes on what you're going to do to your fictional characters. Under these covers, you can keep your sexual escapes alive and your fantasies private, or not. More truth or dare than kiss and tell with its scandalous tips and tricks, this journal will push the boundaries of desire for your fictional characters. Adams Media suggests that you give in to lust, have some fun and write it all down.

Whatever you do, just DON'T leave it on the bus or tube!

The Chicktionary - Words Every Woman Should Know
By Anna Lefler

If you're writing Chick-Lit genre, no doubt you'll be all over the definitions of 'low lights,' 'ruching,' and a 'tankini.' But can you spot a 'Mrs. Potato Head' when you see one?

That's where Anna's *The Chicktionary* comes in. With the help of Anna Lefler and her collection of 450+ must-know words and phrases, you'll be in the know when faced with terms like Aberzombie, Bandeau, George Glass, and Puma.

So whether you are dealing with a Residual Girlfriend, diagnose yourself with a bad case of Basset Knees, or need to go on a Briet, you'll be prepared for all that comes your way.

At the very least, this book will serve as a delightful reminder that everyone has a skeleton in her closet--right next to her fat pants.

If you're not into writing your own *50 Shades of Grey*, and you're thinking of possibly penning a Chick-Lit novel instead, you will love this little 'chick' pink guide to the way some women speak – some are said to have peed themselves laughing.

Take a loo break before you start learning this language.

Look Out For ...

The chapter on dictionaries also gives you a fabulous book on 'slang.' Not that you will write slang, but one of your characters may use slang, which will make them authentic.

Added to my reading list is Kevin Robinson's *218 Facts A Writer Needs To Know About The Police.*

Another book I am dead keen to read is *Making It in Historical Fiction* by Libbie Hawker. If you want to start writing historical fiction this may be the genre learning guide for you. There's no doubt that historical fiction is popular with readers. In fact, the genre is expanding all the time, gaining market share and influencing other media at a rapid pace. But the HF market has some peculiar quirks that can challenge any writer.

I can't wait to read Libbie's advice to ensure my historical novels stack up!

Writing for Children

And above all, watch with glittering eyes the whole world around you because the greatest secrets are always hidden in the most unlikely places. Those who don't believe in magic will never find it. ~ Roald Dahl

How to Write for Children

In my own quest to write a fabulous page-turning book for children, I read lots of books about the art of writing for children and young adults. I am always on the lookout for knowledge that will fuel my inspiration to write a children's novel.

Writing Your Children's Novel

There are so many questions on writing for children; these spring immediately to mind ...

- Which are the best books on writing for children?
- Are there any good courses for writing for children?
- How do you decide what children's age to write for?
- How do you know what's acceptable for certain age children?
- How do you ensure your children's stories are totally unique?
- How do you create your characters?
- Do you write for children you know?
- Do you check your ideas with children before you write?
- Do you ask children for other ideas for your stories?
- Do you prefer to write serious or silly stories for children?
- Where do you research your facts for writing serious children's fiction?

You may be interested in the 2015 *Children's Writer's & Illustrator's Market.* Do what's best for you and your book, and keep up to date with new developments in publishing. It's an exciting time for authors, so make sure you're capitalising on every opportunity.

How to Write for Children and Get Published

By Louise Jordan

Writing for kids is easy, right? We were all kids once and we are surrounded by kids. We know tons of them. Even if you're a hermit hiding in your house writing your self-published books, there'll be kids hanging on your street corner so you can just observe them from a distance. Easy?

No! Children are complex creatures. If you've had one you'll certainly know this to be oh-so-true. Knowing the children's book market is crucial to success as a children's author.

Reading and devouring as many books by children's authors is another must. Knowing which age group to write about and why you want to aim at that age range is also a very essential element.

We want an expert in this area not to tell us prospective children's writers what to do, but to guide us through all the insightful information so that we can write to captivate our children readers.

Enter Louise Jordan ... an expert on writing for children. Louise worked in children's publishing for over twenty-five years and is one of the original founders of The Writers' Advice Centre for Children's Books. Before founding the Advice Centre, Louise worked as head reader for Puffin and still reads for a number of children's publishers, including Puffin, Dorling Kindersley, Ladybird and Warne.

Writing a children's book is not easier than writing an adult book, merely different. What is needed is a clarity of vision, and this is harder than you might think. ~ Louise Jordan

In *How to Write For Children and Get Published*, Louise gives you information from the point of view of both writer and editor, which results in a sympathetic, but pragmatic perspective on the world of children's publishing.

Not only does Louise explore different kinds of books for children of different ages and provide examples of each category, she gears her findings towards the UK market, even though the basic information is universal.

Here you'll learn more about the educational market, young fiction, series reads, reading schemes and general fiction for the different age groups. Along with a section on 'what to write about' Louise gives examples from successful children's fiction authors.

A great example of brainstorming is shown with a spider web of different keywords that could become plot points. Subject matter is covered with a section on all genres and themes of children's fiction. Ending this section, Louise reveals the taboo areas that aspiring novelists should not touch.

The components of a good story include plotting, characterisation, point of view and style. The final section tells writers of children's fiction how to submit work to publishers, and outlines the author's relationship with a publisher once a book is accepted.

Get Writing Children's Fiction
By Karen King

If you need any more ideas, tips and exercises for writing your Children's Fiction novel then dip into *Get Writing Children's Fiction* by Karen King. This book is packed full of inspiration, tips and writing exercises for anyone who wants to write children's fiction.

Like me, your head may be full of children's stories. When I walk my puppy Dexter, I find my mind whirling around like a helicopter blade with ideas flying in every direction. But will they fit together well enough to make an entire readable, page-turning book?

Karen starts off her book on writing for children by giving new children's authors the do's and don'ts of writing for children. She goes through (in great depth) the differences between writing for children and writing for adults, and explains how to write for different genres and age groups.

Then Karen gives you loads of places to get your children's book ideas, as well as suggestions for creating believable characters' children will really relate to so that they'll want to keep their noses stuck in your book.

She also guides you through how to develop plots that keep your readers hooked and she finishes with how to present your work professionally. Throughout the book there are useful links and tips from other published writers.

Chapters include the following:

- Know-how: the difference between writing for children and writing for adults.
- How to get ideas for your stories from your family, your work and your life - and how to expand those ideas.
- Creating believable characters' children will love reading about.
- Writing by the seat of your pants, or plotting? Basic things you need to know for either approach.
- Writing realistic dialogue.
- Writing the first draft; how to create 'reel them in' beginnings, sustain the pace in the middle, and write satisfying endings.
- How to write page-turning chapter endings; keeping continuity when writing a series.

- Writing for the educational market. Writing a synopsis and a proposal. Submitting your work to a publisher or agent.

- Dealing with rejects and rewrites. Publicity and marketing. Publishing your own work.

While Karen is an experienced writing tutor and university lecturer on professional and university writing courses, she has also been writing children's books since the mid-eighties. She's written for many children's magazines including *Sindy*, *Barbie*, *Winnie the Pooh* and *Thomas the Tank Engine*.

Some of her short stories were featured on BBC's Playdays and her poems on the BBC One Potato, Two Potato website. She writes for all ages and in all genres: story books, picture books, plays, joke books, she's written them all!

She currently tutors for The Writer's Bureau and was one of the authors of their 'Writing for Children' course and the author of their 'Write for Profit using the Internet' course. So with all that experience behind writing for children, you'll find examples from her own books sprinkled in amongst the chapters.

As I have already said, I am a huge collector of writing reference guides to help me with my own writing, so I truly appreciate having a book that covers all the topics I want to learn about, in particular - writing for children from start to finish.

The chapters are not long or complex, so you will get through them pretty easily with no scratching of your head trying to make out what Karen is explaining.

Like many of my other treasured books on writing, there are stacks of sticky post-it-notes sticking out in places that I want to go back and re-read. When I am writing my next children's book I will pop back time and time again to remind myself of the learning from this nifty little guide on writing for children.

Picture Writing for Children and Teens

By Anastasia Suen

In this book, successful children's book author Anastasia Suen will guide every self-published writer through creating pictures in your young readers' minds. Here is another fab writing reference guide from the experts over at Writers' Digest.

With 'Picture Writing,' she shows writers how to use descriptive language to create vivid image-stories for kids. Whether you like 'Try It Yourself Exercises' or not, the words of advice from a successful author on how to write books that will captivate a child's imagination is certainly worth having in your writing reference library.

Anastasia starts by explaining the left and right brain process and how one side is literal and the other is visual. So, armed with this insight, you can start to turn your words into pictures. Of course, all these valuable nuggets of advice on the techniques of writing can be applied to adult books as well.

Once you have finished this comprehensive guide on writing children's fiction, you will probably understand why you loved the books you read when you were young. Those are more than likely the kind of books that made you SEE the story through pictures in your mind.

As writers, we all want our readers to keep turning the pages, and one explosive way to do that is by creating vivid pictures in the reader's mind. This doesn't mean just pictures of the setting, but pictures of the hero of your story and other characters.

Anastasia tells writers that by showing details through Picture Writing rather than direct statements, you will be pulling your reader into your story. Who your character is and what he or she wants is your story.

This expert writing tutor says, 'The difference between showing and telling is the difference between scene and summary. Scene shows a picture you can see. Summary uses the author's words to tell you something about the story.'

The mental pictures suggested by the words show readers your characters.

How do readers see, hear, touch, taste and smell the pictures in your story? Go through your chapters and do a checklist on this, scene by scene. Find where you are merely telling the story and turn it into a showing story with vivid pictures for the reader to conjure up in their mind.

Writing Young Adult Fiction

Online Course by Steve Alcorn and Dani Alcorn

Do you have a toy box of bright and fun ideas tumbling through your mind? Ideas that may be good for children's books or more advanced, thrilling stories for young adults (commonly called 'YA Fiction')?

But what exactly is YA Fiction?

Young adult fiction is fiction written for, published for, or marketed to adolescents and young adults, around the ages of 13 to 21 (although interestingly, more than half of all the YA novels sold are bought by adults 18 or older).

Young adult fiction, whether in the form of novels or short stories, has distinct characteristics that distinguish it from the other age categories of fiction. In this fantastic Young Adult Fiction online writing workshop, you will discover everything you need to know to craft your own finished, best-selling YA novel or screenplay! Most importantly, you will learn how to captivate the hearts and minds of Young Adult Readers!

Young Adult Fiction Writing Workshop

This online writing course focuses on Young Adult Fiction Writing, and you will discover exactly why young adult novels are today's most exciting genre. By the end of this training you will know how to use the techniques of top-selling authors to construct your own finished, best-selling novel or screenplay that will rival *Harry Potter, Hunger Games,* or *Twilight!*

Now, what makes this course different from any other course out there is that this isn't just a collection of ideas or principles. It's a proven, step-by-step FORMULA created and delivered right to your screen by two successful young adult fiction writers with a proven track-record of helping others achieve success. This engaging 14-module course gives you all the tools you need to create your own bestseller.

A Writing Course for Any Writer

This course is one of the best writing courses I have taken. The detail on structuring a novel is fantastic. Steve and Dani Alcorn, who run the course, start by exploring young adult fiction and explaining how to plan your writing project. Then they move on to planning young adult projects, where they go through lots of bestselling Young Adult Fiction examples, including resources materials (each module has both examples and resources to download).

From there, Steve and Dani jump into the middle substance of the course. The subject of 'How to Structure your Novel' has several modules dedicated to this subject with lots of detailed sub-topics within each module. Next up is writing your manuscript and polishing your manuscript, and they top it all off with getting published.

Structuring Your Young Adult Novel

This course is one of the best writing courses around - the detail on structuring a novel is fantastic! This section is so intense and detailed and so extremely thorough and well planned that this Young Adult Fiction Writing Workshop is a great resource for every aspiring novelist and writer.

In this section, you will learn how to put all your planning and research and fictional character profiles together into a structure that will keep your readers turning the pages! If you pay close attention to the examples of the details I mention above, such as scene and sequel, you will have the tools to enhance all of your self-published novels, not just your manuscripts for children's or young adult stories.

Not only will the course help to improve your planning and research of your children's and YA fiction, it will also arm you with all the ammo you need to create memorable characters, exciting plots and vivid settings.

If you want to get cracking and whip your novels into shape before you can self-publish them, you really, really need to take this course. It is a serious must-do for all writers of Young Adult Fiction, Children's Fiction and, in fact, any genre!

The full course is run on videos with Steve and Dani chatting through their experience and knowledge on this genre with notes and downloads for each module. You can jump in at any point, but I would recommend that you start at the beginning and go through each module so you don't miss any of their sound expert advice.

Then later, when you want to re-focus your thoughts on a particular topic, jump back into the module on that subject at any time - this course has a lifelong membership.

I also suggest you take notes on each module. I set up a folder for the course and made notes to go with the resource downloads of each module. That way I can jump back to review my notes when needed. As an example, just the other day during another great online course I took on *Writing the Paranormal Novel,* I remembered something Steve had said, so I dived into the folder to find the notes I had made.

I then used the knowledge from this Young Adult Fiction Workshop to apply to an assignment I had to do on the other course when I handed in a supernatural scene. Ta-dah! Each course complemented the other.

Learning About Writing for Young Adults

Here's just a taste of what you'll discover on this course:

- What makes great young adult fiction.
- How to plan your project quickly and easily.
- The most effective way to structure your story.
- Listening to the voices of youth.
- The viewpoints that work best for young adults.
- Experimenting with tense.
- Creating a vibrant narrative voice.
- Building vivid settings.
- Writing dialogue for young adults.
- Meeting your young protagonist.
- Writing effective beginnings and endings.

- Developing a writing style for young adults.
- Techniques for polishing your manuscript like a pro.
- Understanding the cover art that sells young adult fiction novels.
- How to get published.
- How to market your work for maximum sales.

In addition to the video tutorials and panel discussions, the course includes extensive supplemental materials, featuring reference lists, exercises, checklists, and handy reference sheets. Find out more about the course here: http://bit.ly/1LbYq5j

Writing Story Books for Children

Another online course I took was *Writing Story Books for Children*. Modules include 'Getting started' - which talks about the 3 Cs in story structure: Contrast, Conflict, Character. If like me, you love learning more about creating fictional characters, this module will tick all your people-creating boxes.

The course then moves on to age groups and story types and choosing and developing your setting, with each page being a slide show type presentation that you go along at your own pace. Then you get into developing credible characters and writing dialogue for children's fiction.

As always, I enjoy the topic of plotting, storyline and theme and this online writing course for children states that there are five essential page turning elements:

- Planning
- Setting
- Viewpoint
- Plotting
- Characterisation

I won't go into the details, only to say that this section will certainly help any writers new to children's fiction, especially if you tend to devour all the writing advice you can get your hands on to help improve your fiction writing. The advice in this section is bound to help you produce a successful novel.

How to Determine Children's Age Groups

I found the module on age groups valuable so I was dead-keen to get to the modules named 'Writing for the under 7's' and 'Writing for 7 to 12 year olds' and 'Writing for teenagers.'

The module 'Writing fantasy and science fiction' gives you the basics on how writing fantasy differs from writing science fiction and writing paranormal stories.

You can also download the bonus library of resources for learning how to write for children, as your login will be valid for your lifetime.

If you're thinking about writing for children, you probably want to take up an online writing course such as Write Story Books for Children.

For more information hop over to:

http://www.writestorybooksforchildren.com

Look Out For ...

Look at Steve Alcorn's other writing courses at WritingAcademy.com

Writing a Thriller

To produce a mighty book, you must choose a mighty theme.
~ Herman Melville

Technically, thrillers fall under Genre Writing. But I love thrillers so much and have read so many excellent books on the subject I thought it worthy of its own chapter.

When I wrote a post on why we humans loved to be scared, I realised that millions of people don't like reading thrillers because they don't like to be scared. But many more millions abso-loot-ly love to be scared. Not just scared, but having the pants scared off them.

We'd have to see a shrink to fully understand why we love having our insides twisted and turned and why we love escaping with our fictional characters into suspense filled plots and dark, spooky locations.

For me, there is no other feeling like it!

Why Do We Love to Be Scared?

Why do we humans love to be scared? Is it because we want to triumph over evil? Or possibly that delicious moment of catharsis, that release of strong emotions.

In our daily lives, most of us don't have a way to release that kind of emotion or to escape into that kind of world. It's not that we are constantly focused on releasing our pent-up fears. But when we get the chance, there's a tremendous and immediate benefit.

Being scared and then experiencing the ... ahh, catharsis moment. Nothing better!

Learning How to Write a Killer Thriller

In all the craft of writing books I have read and reviewed on my writing blog, U Self-Publish, I gain so much knowledge and understanding of what makes an excellent novel. More to the point here, how to write a killer thriller.

> *Suspense is like a coil. It must get tighter and tighter. And danger and menace gets greater. Take these elements and put them on steroids.* ~ *James Scott Bell*

For novelists writing a conspiracy thriller, it is vital to have these lessons branded on your brain.

Foundations of a Thriller

James Scott Bell believes the core of the thriller is What if? That is the question that should constantly be on your mind as you follow his basic 'foundations of a thriller':

- Death stakes: Physical, Professional or Psychological
- Unforgettable characters
- Organic action
- Increasing tension
- Page turning compulsion

With those elements you will need to add the voice, the style, the spice, the dialogue. Then start raising the stakes, be it personal or societal. With personal stakes: ask the question, how can things get worse? At whatever point you are, what type of event could happen that could make the situation worse, then go a step further and ask, what else could make it even worse than that. Step by step, it becomes a descent into greater and greater trouble.

With societal stakes, work your way out from where they live, their home, their town. Is the trouble snowballing into a greater societal or communal danger? For example, in *The Da Vinci Code*, Dan Brown masterfully shows mounting conspiracy and unravelling of the mystery and the huge ramifications.

Page Turning Compulsions

Once you have a great plot idea, the next step is to marry it to unforgettable characters who are unpredictable and passionate. They must care about something so much that their blood is always pulsing powerfully through their veins. They must also be resourceful and figure out how to survive using every experience and skill they possess.

Suspense is a technique tied to reader's primal instincts and fears. Your job as a writer is to unsettle your readers.
~ Jessica Page Morrell

Of course, the characters you create must be complex, with more than one layer and inner conflict. For heroes to be real and human, an ongoing argument with their inner voices must be there on the page so that you have created sympathy in your readers. Thus we bond with them.

They must also be gutsy. Despite their fear, they go forward. Lastly, they should have a wound, some kind of thing from their past that haunts them in the present.

James says the 'Fear Factor' is a great friend of yours as a writer. He suggests that authors pause before writing a scene to consider what is the fear factor and fear thermometer, and what level they are in that scene. Then find new levels of fear to put your fictional character through.

Something Unexpected in Every Scene

For each scene use SUES:

- Something
- Unexpected
- (in) Every
- Scene

One key to page turning fiction is the unexpected. If readers can predict what is going to happen, they won't turn the page. But if unexpected happens, they are kept on the hook. Every now and then stop and ask yourself: what will your reader expect to happen in this scene? And then do something else using 'Twists and Turns.'

James's Page Turning Compulsion:

1. Action = end scene when bad things happen or seem about to happen
2. Emotion = leave character at the height of emotion

3. Dialogue = end with something that holds intrigue or creates more unease

Bestselling author Sandra Brown says a great thriller is when you build in a secret in every book and keep it until the end to reveal it. She also advocates that authors ask a question in the first scene and answer it in the last scene.

Building and Sustaining Suspense

Jodie Renner believes we must sustain the suspense. To do that, authors must build tension and intrigue, and. they must use foreshadowing for maximum reader involvement.

In her book, *Writing a Killer Thriller,* she offers authors devices for amping up the tension and suspense to delay and tease and stretch out the moment. All the while withholding information and shoving twists and surprises and revelations under your reader's nose.

Jodie believes we must 'Knock 'Em Dead with a Kick-Ass Climax' to create a memorable and satisfying ending.

Thrill Seekers

So, with all this in mind, I decided to create an infographic to keep reminding me of these excellent learning tips:

1. Bang ~ action, reaction and pace sets off the first chapter
2. Big Question ~ first scene and answered in last
3. Secrets ~ only revealed at end
4. Killer Plot Surprises ~ something unexpected in every scene
5. Cliffhanging and Jump Cut Pace ~ page turning compulsion, can't put the book down
6. Suspense ~ foreshadowing keeps them intrigued

7. Complex Characters ~ memorable to readers
8. Conflict Stakes ~ personal and societal issues
9. Ticking Clock ~ give your characters a deadline, a race against time and then shorten the timetable
10. Climax big fight scenes ~ darken the character's last few moments of the book to give the reader a big pay-off

Find out why humans love to be scared ~ just by reading a thriller!

Writing Scary Scenes

By Rayne Hall

If you love to scare your readers, and you're writing a thriller, crime novel, a mystery or any other piece of fiction that requires you to write a scary scene, you need to read Rayne Hall's eBook *Writing Scary Scenes*, which will guide you through the process of creating fast paced scary scenes.

Once you open Rayne's eBook, you will quickly learn practical tricks to turn up the suspense in your thriller or horror novel. Rayne teaches you how to make your readers' hearts hammer with suspense, their breaths quicken with excitement, and their skins tingle with goosebumps of delicious fright.

I couldn't get enough of learning how to write scary scenes filled with suspense.

I don't just want to read it and retain it, I want it to soak into my skin and ooze out of my fingers when they type up my scary thrilling scenes. I want all this juicy scary stuff to float around me so it can jump off my novel pages and scare the hell out of my readers!

Suspense is a feeling – the feeling of excitement, of tension, of fear, the feeling of needing to know what happens next. As writers, we aim to create suspense, because our readers love it. ~ Rayne Hall

With stacks of scary books under her belt, and writing Fantasy Fiction along with Horror Fiction, Rayne's author motto is: Dark * Dangerous * Disturbing.

Are Your Frightening Scenes Scary Enough?

With many chapters aimed at scaring your readers, Rayne guides you through the process of writing tight, fast-paced action scenes that thrill and chill your readers. That's the reason they're reading your novel after all. Rayne offers practical suggestions such as ...

- How to structure a scary scene
- How to increase the suspense
- How to make the climax more terrifying
- How to have your reader feel the character's fear
- Techniques for manipulating the readers' subconscious
- Creating powerful emotional effects

If you have written your book and need help to scary it up, you should use this book to write a new scene, or to add tension and excitement to a new draft. My suggestion would be to read the book and then create your own scene checklist based on the info you have gleaned and learned from Rayne's writing experience. And then keep your checklist handy while writing your scary scenes.

You will learn tricks of the trade for your novel's 'black moment' and your ultimate 'climax' scenes. Along with finding out how to describe monsters and villains and learning the best methods for writing harrowing captivity sections and breathtaking escapes, there are chapters on instant hooks, how to isolate your hero, how to use senses and ensure that your readers feel the same fear as the hero.

You'll also learn which 'flavours of fear' you should inject into your different scenes. The handy thing here is that Rayne gives you 'Drawbacks' in each chapter - so where she tells you how to create all this scary stuff, she also advises you when you should go easy and why.

This is important in writing scary scenes, not only because you don't want to go OTT, but you also don't want to put your reader off or have your scenes come across as unbelievable.

It goes without saying that *Writing Scary Scenes* is the ideal writing guide for all genres, especially thriller, horror, paranormal romance and urban fantasy. Of course, if you are writing any other genre and need a little injection of scary, read and learn from Rayne's writing experience.

Scare the Pants off Your Readers

The first time I picked up the book, I got stuck in it and couldn't put it down; I made stacks of notes and scribbled in the margins. I also marked out so many tips in yellow highlight and then, as I motored through the 26 chapters, eating it alive, suddenly it ended!

I wanted it to go on and on. I wanted more. I needed to learn more. I couldn't get enough of learning how to write scary scenes.

Think of suspense this way: If conflict is the engine of fiction, then suspense is the fuel that makes it run. ~ Jessica Page Morrell

As my own novels will one day thrill and scare my readers, Rayne's *Writing Scary Scenes* has joined my ranks of FAV writing guides, alongside how to create fictional characters, how to create emotions for characters, writing dialogue and slang for novel people and many other precious books I have had the pleasure of reviewing.

Writing a thriller with this kind of scare tactics up one's writing sleeve is soooo exciting, especially a suspense conspiracy thriller like *The Grotto's Secret.*

To find out more about Rayne's scary and horrific fiction, pop over to Amazon Central and look for Rayne's books. Or go straight to buy this scary little ebook!

Writing a Killer Thriller

By Jodie Renner

I have to tell you that Jodie's book, *Writing a Killer Thriller,* completely and utterly shaped my thriller writing. And I can see PROOF of this in the beta reader feedback of my first novel: *The Grotto's Secret.* The exact techniques Jodie teaches in this book are coming up trumps with very positive comments from my beta readers.

For example, they loved my 'jump cuts' and leaving them hanging (and worrying) by going off into another character's head straight after a cliff hanger; again, this is something Jodie teaches you to do.

One reader reported that it was exciting and exhilarating bouncing between my characters and their time-lines (one medieval, one modern day) as well as jumping back to each of their baddies.

Fiction is about characters that readers are intimately involved with and worried about. ~ Jessica Page Morrell

In addition to these tips, Jodie goes through the different ways you can structure your story plot and shows you how to bring your characters to life on the page.

The chapters that I found fantastic and extremely helpful to a new novelist were the chapters on how to build tension and suspense. They place a big emphasis on foreshadowing, which tends to keep your reader's nose buried in your book. Isn't that what all aspiring authors want?!

Twists, delays, withholding information, teasing and stretching the suspense are all vital parts of a thriller, and Jodie makes it all look so simple. And it is; with Jodie's book beside me, I wrote my historical conspiracy thriller - I can't wait to see more reader reactions.

I have lots of Post it notes sticking out of *Writing a Killer Thriller*, and I often jump to them for guidance and reminders. I could write pages and pages of excellent praise, but I think you will gain much more if you read the book as soon as you can get your hands on a copy, especially if you are writing a thriller.

Definitely one of the best writing resource books on my bookshelf!

Writing the Thriller

By T. Macdonald Skillman

This author starts by defining suspense and knowing what type of suspense to write. She breaks thrillers down into several key categories and then explores each category in greater detail.

In the section on characterisation in thrillers, she explores topics such as 'bringing characters to life,' 'how to describe viewpoint characters without using mirrors,' 'avoiding stereotypes' and 'why even villains need a soft spot'.

She goes through plotting and setting up a thrilling atmosphere with different points of view and back story. She also discusses how secrets, threats and moments of panic or terror can raise the stakes. For example:

'I have your son.'

These four simple words would strike terror into any parent's heart.

Along with dialogue, pacing and themes, you will go through how to write the perfect ending for your thriller, and what works and why.

At the end of this book there are interviews with authors who have had success in writing suspense in different thriller genres.

What Is Suspense?

Rayne's quick trick for increasing the suspense: Let your protagonist walk through a doorway on her way to danger.

A recipe of suspense is made up of curiosity, uncertainty and anxiety. ~ Jessica Page Morrell

Slow the story's pace for a moment and linger at the door. Describe the door: Is it dark oak, grimy glass, gleaming steel, or splintering hardwood with peeling paint?

Are there any danger clues, such as knife marks, smashed glass, ominous stains, thorny plants, perhaps even a sign 'Visitors Unwelcome' or 'Keep Out' nailed to the centre?

Describe the sound of the doorbell, or the weight of the keys in her hand. Finally, describe how the door opens.

By the time your protagonist steps through the door, the reader's suspense is turned to high volume, intensely anticipating what happens next.

If you want to increase the suspense further still, describe the sound of the door as it closes behind her. For example: The door snapped shut.

Read Rayne's blog to explore ideas about suspense and thrills lurking behind doors

The Sceptic's Guide to Conspiracies
By Monte Cook

From the Knights Templar to the JFK Assassination, Monte Cook uncovers the truth behind the world's most controversial and covered-up conspiracy theories in his writing guide called *The Sceptics Guide to Conspiracies.*

The Sceptic's Guide to Conspiracies takes the reader through the major conspiracy theories that abound in the world - from the historically complex to the seriously whacked out. This work features entries that include a description of the theory, evidence for and against it, and prominent figures associated with it.

Rather than using this book as a serious exploration of conspiracy theories, use it to get inspiration for your own conspiracy theories when you start writing your thriller novel.

The back cover is covered with scribbles in red ink warning you about secrets and who's calling the shots. There are also various hand-scribbled comments in more red ink in the margins on every page. It's all quite funny and light-hearted.

Pop over to Amazon, and you'll see that some other reviewers have slated the theories as insane theories, but do remember that Monte Cook is bringing you a 'Sceptic's Guide,' not hard facts. I believe it is meant to be a light, entertaining read for readers and writers' of thrillers who could be inspired by some of the conspiracy ideas mentioned.

If nothing else, the 'Conspiracy Run Down' should inspire novelists setting out on a thriller-writing journey, with links for further reading on the web and search terms to let your mind go mad with plot points and a who's who checklist so you know which organisations or associations to explore.

Use this book as a not-so-serious writing guide to finding inspiration for improving your thriller writing. I did, and have now got my very own historical conspiracy thriller, *The Grotto's Secret.*

Writing Dark Stories
By Rayne Hall

Although Rayne suggests this eBook is for short stories or novellas, I think you could use the themes to inspire ideas for your thriller.

For example, in the chapter called 'Feed Your Fiction with Your Fears,' you are given ideas for dark places and how to use weird shudders and phobias or childhood fears and dreams to plot story lines.

Rayne also covers all kinds of dark genres, such as mystery, supernatural, paranormal, fantasy, gothic, ghost stories and of course, horror.

Building suspense and managing tension are important aspects of a dark story, along with raising the stakes and conflicts among your characters.

All these topics (and more) are included in Rayne's dark little eBook, jam packed with creepy ideas.

Look Out For ...

Here's a reminder of the download link which includes my Thrill Seekers Infographic: http://eepurl.com/bC_vjX

And finally you'll get to know about the surprise I mentioned way back in the first chapter on story structure. Keep reading ...

Blueprints

I'm sure all new novelists learning the art of writing will jump at the chance of finding a blueprint, a document intended as a guide for creating their next novel.

Well, some of these fabulous writing tutors I have been telling you about have done just that. In this chapter we'll go through some inspirational writing guides that provide templates for writing different aspects of your novel.

Read these books for a model or outline to follow and adapt when writing your novel. By no means am I suggesting that you write a predictable, cookie-cutter or formulaic story. I am suggesting you read some (most or preferably all) of these excellent writing guides listed up till now. Then, all fired up and totally inspired, you read the ones we are about to cover because they will guide you with basic templates to get your story written.

Remember, a blueprint is an outline. You have to work out all the inside parts. You have to mould your characters with all the new information gained from the books I have mentioned, you'll plan, research and plot your story structure and add twists and turns that show your story people passionate about their goals and overcoming high stakes.

To craft a bestseller you need: Blueprints with a bursting imagination and you need to be armed with all the knowledge in your writer's tool kit belt-bag taken from the books we have discussed.

Along with all the books in *Pimp My Fiction*, the following writing resources are aimed to inspire you to write great fiction.

Scene & Structure

By Jack Bickham

We started the first chapter of this book by listing some of the best books on structuring your story. You will remember how I said *Scene & Structure* is an excellent book on structuring your scenes action by action; now you will see how this book also gives you a novel's blueprint.

Story Structure Blue Print

The publisher claims that this book is your 'game plan for success.' I claim that it will become your blueprint for creating a successful novel. Using dozens of examples from his own work, such as Dropshot and Tiebreaker, Jack M. Bickham guides you through building a sturdy framework for your novel.

As you work on crafting compelling scenes that move the reader, moment by moment, toward the story's resolution, you will learn how to end every scene with a disaster - not always an earthquake type of disaster, small plot points can be disasters too.

My novel, *The Grotto's Secret,* and the sequel I am currently writing, *The Sacred Symbol,* are both based on the blueprint template that Jack gives you. If you need a blueprint to write your novel, read this book and study the basic fundamentals of fiction. By time you reach the end, it will all make so much sense.

How to Write Fight Scenes

By Rayne Hall

In Rayne Halls eBook, *How to Write Fight Scenes,* she gives you a template to write your fight scenes.

For example, Rayne details several stages of how to set up your fight scene, including different elements for the location, and she goes on to describe how you can raise the stakes and keep your reader in suspense. Finally, she shows you how to move your fight scene into action with a thrilling climax.

I found this so useful when writing my own fight scenes for my latest novel that I typed out Rayne's fight scene template and used it, along with other valuable notes that I added to each section.

For example, I wanted to have my character fighting in self-defence, so I added that to my 'action' section. I set up my fight scenes to include all Rayne's notes on location and how to ensure a fight scene takes place in a unique place.

The book covers every possible aspect of a fight scene, from weapons to settings to things you couldn't have even imagined would go into a fight scene. This excellent must-read eBook will ensure your fight scenes leap off the page!

In fact, if you combine Rayne's template for fight scenes with her advice and examples from *Writing Vivid Settings*, along with the blueprint from *Scene and Sequel*, you will have a master template for writing your whole novel.

Ta-dah!

45 Master Characters

By Victoria Lynn Schmidt

Using Victoria Lynn Schmidt's archetypes will help you make sense of your characters and their world. It certainly will help you to address, explore and deal with current situations coming out of your plot.

In my chapter on 'Creating Characters,' you will have read about *45 Master Characters*. When you have finished going through all the types of possible characters, why not use one or more of them as a blueprint for creating your next fictional character?

I did this for one of my characters in my novel, and so far my beta readers have commented on this particular character as the character they most enjoyed reading about, who they immediately started worrying about and how they quickly found empathy with her. Who is she?

If you read my conspiracy thriller, *The Grotto's Secret* and *45 Master Characters* and know who I am referring to, please drop me a line via my website or on Twitter (@paulawynne) and I will send you a free copy of my sequel, *The Sacred Symbol*. In all my future novels, I plan to rely on *45 Master Characters* as my blueprint for creating characters.

Write Your Novel in 30 Days

By Karen S. Wiesner

Many aspiring and experienced novelists throw out hundreds of pages (and waste valuable time) before they have a workable first draft of a novel. *With First Draft in 30 Days* those days are over.

But that doesn't give you a good picture of what you're getting with Karen's MUST HAVE book for every aspiring novelist. The back cover tells you how this book will save you time and reduce rewrites with a 'sure-fire system' for creating your first draft.

Although it doesn't have to be actually 30 days – it could be whatever time allocation you want it to be, I found Victoria Schmidt's writing reference guide shows you how to create an outline so detailed and complete that it really does become your first draft.

Her system is flexible enough for you to customise it to your way of researching, planning, plotting and writing.

When you first open the book you may think 'Mmmmm, I don't wanna be tied to any writing formatting system, thanks.' But once you actually start working through Karen's ideas, chapter by chapter, and if you DO follow her guidance you will be amazed; no, astounded; no, stunned; no. bowled over ... oh, you get the picture ... by this revolutionary way to write your first draft.

Using your own approach and style, you will ease into Karen's way of thinking pretty damn quickly, and with her interactive worksheets, you'll have your own process in no time at all.

If you're the kind of writer that I am, flying by the seat of your pants and allowing your fictional characters to speak to you and dictate what happens next, go to Amazon right now and buy this book.

I am warning you that if you don't, you will never know how much your writing can and will be improved. You will see how this way of working not only improves your plotting and structure, but even more so, your actual writing.

Why?

Because when you apply this system to your manuscripts or novel ideas you will see something amazing happening – your writing tightens up, and your story drives forward at a rapid pace.

If you think you don't need an organising structure, especially if you have never done it before, you actually do – you just don't realize it until you get to grip with Karen's steps to write the first draft of your novel.

Along with plotting your novel, you'll see that Karen teaches you how to brainstorm all possible angles for your story and organise the mountains of 'stuff' you could gather during your research and planning.

If you are still resisting, do me a favour, just read three to five chapters and then tell me you still don't agree. At that stage, I will concede that you may be a writer who simply gets a kick out of organised chaos and will manage to get your book written under your own cluttered steam.

But if you do give it a go, you may be like me and find that you're way ahead with your creative outlines than you ever were without them.

Without a doubt, as someone who has written for most of my life and has yet to get a book published, I found Karen's book to be massively inspiring, downright feet-on-the-road useful, and it has helped me to create a novel that is, so far, probably my best work yet. By following her expertise, I have produced a piece of fiction that I am now more determined than ever to get published.

When I am finished with my new novel based entirely on Karen's guidance – and I subsequently get it published as a bestseller, I intend to go back over my previous novels and use the same principles.

If you can only afford one of these great books I have recommended, start with this one!

You will NOT be disappointed. I cannot recommend the book enough for new writers starting out on their novel writing journey!

Scenes Checklist

Earlier I mentioned that I had a little surprise coming up. I have my own Scene Checklist, which has different aspects of creating each and every scene I write about.

Scene structure is one of the most important tools in a writer's toolbox. ~ CS Lakin

I use my Scene Checklist as a kick-start, and then I come back to it at the end to boot my scenes back into a tight order. I have compiled this Checklist organically, as I have read and absorbed much of the awesome advice from the books I have listed. If you'd like to borrow this, you can download my document and use it to create your scenes or start adding your own checkpoints as well. Download my Scenes Checklist here: http://eepurl.com/bC_vjX

If you download my Scene Checklist (and the other documents I mentioned earlier) and you decide to stay on my mailing list I will send you a free copy of the updated version of Pimp My Fiction, which will feature the new books I am currently reading and reviewing. Of course if I find any other great resources I will include those too. After all, writers must stick together and help each other. If you come across anything that you feel will be helpful to the readers of this book, please drop me a line.

Look Out For ...

Here's an idea ~ download Susanne Lakin's check lists that she gives you at the end of each chapter in *The 12 Pillars of Novel Construction* (in case you're hopping about see the chapter on story structure).

Add these to the other templates mentioned above and you have a great starting point for constructing your novel! All the bones are thrown out there in front of you, you just need the creative imagination to start adding fleshy bits to the skeleton.

Gee, isn't it exciting to be a novelist!

Self-Editing

Write. Rewrite. When not writing or rewriting, read. I know of no short cuts ~Larry L. King

Admit it, you hate self-editing. All writers are said to hate this process. It's the creative part of writing or rewriting that gives us the buzz to race to the end.

But whether you are publishing through a traditional publishing contract or self-publishing your novel, you need to do revision and lots of self-editing before handing it over to either an agent or to an editor who will do your final edit.

Revision and Self Editing for Publication

By James Scott Bell

Amazon says that James Scott Bell's book, *Revision and Self Editing for Publication*, is designed to eliminate the intimidation factor that comes with revision and self-editing. But any aspiring novelist or writer, having read this book, will take much more out of it.

First things first. You must have a completed manuscript. And that takes enough elbow grease; creating fictional characters and possibly even reading through a lot of writing reference guides.

Nevertheless, your completed manuscript needs some tarting up. So where do you start? I received this book from the publisher thinking 'Mmm, this will be a quick read. I'll jump here and there through it, just to review the book and make them and the author happy.' Job done.

Like most wannabe writers, I thought my completed novel didn't need another rewrite; it's gone through numerous versions of that already. So why on earth would I need to go through all that pain again?

And then I started reading...

Back in the Creative Groove

When you start reading James' revision book, you get right back into writing mode. You know you have a job ahead of you once you go through his chapters on self-editing: talking about characters, plot and structure, points of view, scenes and dialogue, middles and ends, theme and setting, description and ...

Phew - this job is certainly not done.

Before you can even think of starting the revision process, James gives you techniques to use during the initial writing phase that will minimize the amount of revision that's required. If only I'd had this book right at the start of my writing!

The Ultimate Revision Checklist

As well as giving us aspiring novelists guidelines for creating a damn good book in the first place, James also sets out the philosophy of editing before you revise and explains about the first read-through. He then goes deeper into ... err, deepening the novel, its characters and plots, and comes up trumps with the ultimate revision checklist. This checklist really is a bible for writers who want to get published.

James states early in the book that it helps to write your book's back cover early on; you'll then have a concise summary of your plot firmly in your head so that you can concentrate on the big picture. He even says to write a few crits as if you were a journalist reviewing the book: boast about your book and its characters – after all, only you get to see that part. But the idea here is to really get the nitty gritty into your head to arm you with the task ahead – the rewrite.

This is another book in our writing reference guides that has so much to offer, and I want to share so many inspiring quotes and points I learnt from the book – that I thought I didn't need – but it would spoil it for you.

All I can say is: Don't ever stop your growth as a writer. You need to keep making each book better than the last by creating a plan of attack for strengthening your piece of work.

James guides you with this advice - find the core of the scene with questions like: what's the purpose of the scene and why does the scene exist?

He advocates:

1. Establish viewpoint
2. Ensure conflict in every scene
3. Action scenes must show clear objectives
4. Reaction scenes must show clear emotion

Dialogue speeds up your scene with short, sharp bursts. The white space gives movement. Go back over your scenes and lighten the heavy text to show more white – moving – space. This is not always easily done, but dialogue is a good place to start refreshing those scenes. And of course, dialogue is an excellent way to avoid 'telling.'

Look for scenes where you're telling the reader instead of showing, and turn that into dialogue with action happening all around.

I found that some scenes in my novel (which I thought didn't need a rewrite) were leaning toward the 'telling' department, and turning those scenes into action packed with dialogue strengthened the scenes. Strangely enough, so many other little things fell into place naturally. It was wonderfully cathartic.

Another rewriting technique I am using is raising the stakes, which is exactly where I am now headed. *Revision and Self Editing for Publication* tucked under one arm, reams of notes under the other, and a head full of bubbling ideas for rewriting my novel, I have all the tools and advice I thought I didn't need to transform my first (or maybe fifth or sixth?) draft into a finished manuscript, ready to be sold!

Look Out For ...

Some fabulous software allows you to have your entire novel read back to you. In my opinion, this is an important step in self-editing. You'll find these tools mentioned in the Writing Tools chapter.

Dictionaries and Thesauruses

Oh Dear, have you swallowed a dictionary? ~ Downton Abbey

While you're writing the book that you may (or may not) intend to self-publish, you'll most likely dive into a wide variety of different dictionaries and thesauruses. I wanted to find out the most popular and best dictionary list for writers to keep to hand during the fiction writing process. And of course, the editing thereafter. When you check this list of books on my shelf, you'll think I'm a bit of a dictionary nut!

Along with a list of metaphors and similes to inspire you to find your own unique wording, a Roget's buffet of synonyms to whet the writing appetite is always useful - or perhaps you have a forever friend in the *Collins Pocket English Thesaurus* instead, where the word is listed in red to stand out on the page.

You may prefer the *Chambers Guide to Idioms* to inject phrases into your fictional character's dialogue or the *Chambers Dictionary of Synonyms and Antonyms* with many thousands of A-Z options for word choices. Or maybe you find the *Oxford Dictionary of Modern Slang* useful to making your characters talk like real people.

So where does that all leave you? Too much choice?

How to Choose a Dictionary or Thesaurus

It can be a writing and time challenge to find the perfect fit from the list of dictionaries that may be on your writing shelf as a well-used pal. How do you choose? From the book jacket cover or thumb index tabs, table of contents or a personal recommendation from another writer?

Only you will know what will be the most useful dictionary you can own. It's easy enough finding the most up-to-date dictionary available, but will it be the right one for you and your writing requirements?

You will know what kind of dictionary or thesaurus should sit beside your PC throughout your novel writing process. Before you ask yourself "What it is that I want from a dictionary?" take a look at some that we found - they all suit different purposes in the writing process.

For example, if you're writing fantasy, you may want to dive into *Fantasy and Fables*. Or if you're writing a thriller with a psycho running around, the *Oxford Dictionary of Psychology* will help to deepen not only your mad villain, but your hero too.

I've had fun collecting a list of dictionaries for writers, but if you have one that I absolutely should feature in this book, please drop me a line.

Dictionary of Modern Slang

By John Ayto and John Simpson

There's no end to the 'mind-blowing' power of Modern Slang. As a mouse is electronically wired to a laptop, so too will *The Oxford Dictionary of Modern Slang* become an intravenous drip to a writer.

Character Labels

Not only can you find modern ways with dialogue, but you can create sparkling 'labels' for your characters. Have a good nose through the thematic section, it's like bottled inspiration!

Don't give a boring account of a man with no hair. Bald is out. Slaphead is in – especially if you want him to be a ruffian or dodgy character. For example, when describing your suspect … let's call him Mike … why write 'Mike was bald' when you could scribe 'a slaphead in a three piece suit'? Why give another character 'big eyes' when they can have 'lamps' … or they may have 'peepers' for that matter.

Your teens or young guns wouldn't say 'this room stinks.' More likely they would grunt out a 'this joint is minging.' If you had to kill off a character for whatever reason, why would they be just 'dead' when they could be 'pushing up daisies'?

People Power

Take a look at the section on 'People and Society'; here you have a wide choice of words to describe folks from different nations, and depending on the character, you may want a bad ass to say something derogatory or lightly refer to their ethnic group.

Same with people status, a child wouldn't be simply a child. Depending on who the character is that is referring to the child, they could be a sprog, a sprout, a rug-rat or a squirt.

Whether you are describing a posh totty or a down and out tramp, *Modern Slang* feeds you a smorgasbord of juicy bang on trend jargon.

And when you get to create a villain and write his or her dialogue, you have a multitude of sins to make their dialogue bounce of the page and into the hearts and minds of your readers. If one of your characters is having it out with a fat person, they could lob any number of lippy expressions from the chocker A to Z, which packs most of the book.

Global Trot

For extra value, *this dictionary* even gives you the time period of the slang, such as 'green-ass - adjective. U.S. Inexperienced. 1949.' In most cases *Modern Slang* helps you out with suggestions on use, such as 'grasser -noun (1950): Five minutes alone with you and he'll be babbling like a grasser (1968).'

Much of the slang listings also give you ethnic origins such as African-American or Austral, and you'll even find quotes from popular publications such as 'ankle-biter, noun, Austral, a young child. 1981. *Sydney Morning Herald.* Travelling overseas with an ankle-biter has its advantages.'

Don't stop at the people suggested in the themes; follow through to build your hero or baddie through the different categories. Find inventive and attention-grabbing descriptors such a 'beanpole' or 'lofty' rather than tall, and drop in 'lard-ass' to replace the well-known fatty. And maybe an 'anorak' for someone obsessed with something, and try 'loaded' for your down and out drunk.

Include behaviour and employment in a character's point of view – for example they may earn 'peanuts' or 'chicken-feed,' they may be a scientist … err preferably a boff, perhaps they graft or schlep as a sparky, they could be a sob-sister or wet leg and their mood today could be 'gutted' or 'creased up.' Instead of young or old, they could be described as a snot-nose or rookie and a wrinkly or codger. There are also lots and lots of rude examples dishing out some game on chat for your characters to be vulgar!

Earbashing the Johns

As all good reviews go, I need to cover both the good and bad. Quite simply, there is no bad with this book, but I still give the two Johns an ear-bashing. This dictionary was first published in 1997 and the second edition in 2008. My only beef, and it's not so much a beef – more like a plea – is that the two Johns should turn this into a Roget's of Modern Slang. Why? So that us mere mortals of aspiring writers are hand-held and nourished through the process of trying to find these scintillating ideas for dialogue and character descriptions.

For example, you may know that your bitchy femme fatale who wheedles money out of an innocent man is a gold-digger, and you'd find her pretty easily under G, but what if you were struggling to fathom out a label for your gawky, awkward middle-aged anti-social man? You may not find him under K for klutz.

Just as *Roget's Thesaurus* sections words in the endless index and then gives section numbers to find a variety of words in themes such as 'Matter in General' or 'Emotion' and 'Intellect', I think *Modern Slang* deserves a similar format.

So back to our klutz: he could be mentioned under gawky and awkward, or he could rear his head under many other descriptors, and thus the intrepid new writer will inevitably trip over the klutz at some point of poring over their 'Roget's of Modern Slang'! The whole idea for a writer to be thumbing through the book is to find slang they don't know, so how do they know where to find it if they don't know the slang exists?

Stacks more work for the Johns of course; I know this because I keep my own personal document of hip-hop-happening dialogue slang I came across, but they're already old sweat at the game so it should be abso-bloody-lutely on their to do list!

Help Us Writers, O Mighty Publisher

Also a note to their publisher, Oxford University Press (OUP): it would be super-duper for writers to have the Thematic Index in the contents marked by page number (s) – just helps a busy writer 'legit' to the 'hot spot' as 'quick as poss.'

Ok, now that I've been a douche-bag and given the boys grief, it doesn't mean this dictionary is in the dog-house. By no means! It will proudly be da-bomb, causing a doodah beside Roget's, its bro dictionaries from OUP, and my other dog-eared writing reference guides.

Every writer should devour this dialogue treasure trove to ensure their characters' dialogue is packed with human oomph. A writer's addiction!

Similes Dictionary

By Elyse Sommer

Using similes will bring your writing to life: they create a visual picture in the mind of your reader and allow them to imagine your scene exactly as you do.

The Similes Dictionary is packed with more than 16,000 imaginative, colourful phrases such as 'quiet as an eel swimming in oil' and 'as plentiful as blackberries' to inspire readers.

With examples from more than 2,000 sources such as the Bible, Shakespeare, and Socrates as well as popular films, TV shows and music, the *Similes Dictionary* covers hundreds of subjects broken into thematic categories that include happiness, anger, virtue, age, ambition, importance and youth, helping readers find the fitting phrase quickly and easily.

Metaphors Dictionary

By Elyse Sommer with Dorrie Weiss

A masterful metaphor, like a picture, may be worth a thousand words. By comparing two unlike objects or ideas, it illuminates the similarities between them, accomplishing in a word or phrase what could otherwise be expressed only in many words, if at all.

This title offers a collection of 6,500 colourful contemporary comparative phrases.

Like the *Similes Dictionary,* you may want to leaf through this for inspiration on creating beautiful metaphors that come from your character's point of view.

Dictionary of Similes, Metaphors and Expressions
By Surendra Sahu

This book is an alphabetical arrangement of more than 140 words such as 'air,' 'man,' 'love' and similes and metaphors with conjunctions such as 'as,' 'than' and 'like.' Works from more than a hundred of the greatest American, European and Nobel Prize winning authors are included.

This dictionary is an invaluable reference book for students of literature and linguistics, as well as average readers who simply appreciate the beauty of language.

The Positive Trait Thesaurus
By Angela Ackerman and Becca Puglisi

It's a writer's job to create compelling characters who can withstand life's fallout without giving up. But building authentic, memorable heroes is no easy task. To forge realistic characters, we must hobble them with flaws that set them back while giving them positive attributes to help them achieve their goals. So how do writers choose the right blend of strengths for their characters—attributes that will render them admirable and worth rooting for—without making it too easy for them to succeed?

Character creation can be hard, but it's about to get a lot easier. Inside *The Positive Trait Thesaurus*, you'll find a large selection of attributes to choose from when building a personality profile.

If you find character creation difficult or worry that your cast members all seem the same, *The Positive Trait Thesaurus* is brimming with ideas to help you develop one-of-a-kind, dynamic characters that readers will love. Extensively indexed, with entries written in a user-friendly list format, this brainstorming resource is perfect for any character creation project.

The Negative Trait Thesaurus

By Angela Ackerman and Becca Puglisi

Crafting likeable, interesting characters is a balancing act, and finding that perfect mix of strengths and weaknesses can be difficult. But the task has become easier, thanks to *The Negative Trait Thesaurus*. Through its flaw-centric exploration of character arc, motivation, emotional wounds, and basic needs, writers will learn which flaws make the most sense for their heroes, villains, and other members of the story's cast.

This book's vast collection of flaws will help writers to explore the possible causes, attitudes, behaviours, thoughts, and related emotions behind their characters' weaknesses so they can be written effectively and realistically.

Common characterization pitfalls, and methods for avoiding them, are also included, along with invaluable downloadable tools to aid in character creation. Written in list format and fully indexed, this brainstorming resource is perfect for creating deep, flawed characters that readers will relate to.

Writer's Descriptive Word Finder

By Barbara Ann Kipfer

Another favourite of mine. When in full writing flow, I try not to disturb my stream of conscious if I need better word alternatives. I just type in a note to myself so I can get all my thoughts down on the page. Later I come back to the notes and then go digging for better words.

This book comes in handy because it's a unique combination of dictionary and thesaurus devoted exclusively to adjectives, with thousands of entries for describing people, places and things.

Even better, it's organised by themes under specific category headings, making it fun to poke around looking for word choices. By hopping in and out of the references, you can add nuance and originality to your fiction.

If you're looking to keep your manuscript fresh and evocative, the less-familiar adjectives offer you many colourful and rich terms that will add flavour to your novel. You can turn to this resource whether you want to encourage adjectives to creep into your writing, use this book as inspiration or take words directly from the word finder. You choose.

Oxford Dictionary of Psychology

By Andrew M. Colman

If you're writing about characters in your novel then the *Oxford Dictionary of Psychology* should definitely be on your bookcase to help you get to grips with the complex workings of the mind.

With over 11,000 authoritative and up-to-date entries, this best-selling dictionary covers all branches of psychology, including psychoanalysis, psychiatry, criminology, neuroscience, and statistics.

It features comprehensive coverage of key areas, for example: cognition, sensation and perception, emotion and motivation, learning and skills, language, mental disorder, and research methods. Entries provide clear and concise definitions, word origins and derivations, and are extensively cross-referenced for ease of use. Over 80 illustrations complement the text.

The section on Phobias and phobic stimuli is a great way to add flaws to your fictional characters. Browse through the list to give your novel's people all kinds of weird things that make them come alive on the page with real-life, flourishing issues.

Dictionary of World Mythology (Oxford)

By Arthur Cotterell

Since Plato first coined the term 'mythologia,' mythology has come to hold greater significance and power as a crucial element of civilization as a whole. Written by a leading scholar of ancient civilizations, the *Oxford Dictionary of World Mythology* presents the powerful gods of Greece, Rome, and Scandinavia, the more mystical deities of Buddhist and Hindu India, and the stern spirits of the African and American continents.

Drawing upon hundreds of myths from around the globe, it not only reveals the vast differences in these civilizations, but also demonstrates the unity of mankind in its fundamental need for explanations of the unknown.

If you're writing science fiction or fantasy, you'll want to dive into this dictionary. Not just for ideas and inspiration, but to gain some knowledge on the history of myths going back yonks and yonks. You can look at old myths and make up your own, inspired from historical Greek gods or any number of other beings listed in this handy guide for fantasy writers.

Dictionary of Foreign Words and Phrases
From OUP Oxford

This updated and revised edition is the authoritative guide to foreign words and phrases often used in contemporary British and American English. Drawn from over 40 languages, the 6,000 entries detail the history of each word or phrase and provide selected quotations to clearly illustrate their use in the English language.

Authors of all genres of writing are subject to being pulled into this book. Whether you're writing a romance and need some French lovey-dovey phrases or writing a killer thriller with a ruthless villain from any given country in the world, you can nose through this dictionary to spice up your dialogue or narrative with foreign words.

Dictionary of Reference & Allusion (Oxford)
By Andrew Delahunty

Allusions form a colourful extension to the English language, drawing on our collective knowledge of literature, mythology, and the Bible to give us a literary shorthand for describing people, places, and events. So a cunning crook is an Artful Dodger, a daydreamer is like Billy Liar, a powerful woman is a modern-day Amazon - we can suffer like Sisyphus, fail like Canute, or linger like the smile of the Cheshire Cat.

This absorbing and accessible A to Z catalogue explains the meanings of allusions in modern English, from Adonis to Zorro, Tartarus to Tarzan, and Rubens to Rambo. Fascinating to browse through, the book is based on an extensive reading programme that has identified the most commonly-used allusions.

This new edition of the *Oxford Dictionary of Reference & Allusion* includes within each entry a short definition for the allusion or reference, ideal for quick reference, and at least one illustration from a wide range of source materials in almost every entry: from Aldous Huxley to Philip Roth, Emily Brontë to *The Guardian Unlimited*. A useful thematic index allows searching for allusions related to a specific topic, e.g. under Intelligence find Aristotle, Einstein, and Spock; and under Hair find Medusa, Samson, and Shirley Temple.

Dictionary of Phrase and Fable

From OUP Oxford

Who? What? Where? Why? This book provides information about the stories behind words, names, and sayings. It covers classical and other mythologies, history, religion, folk customs, superstitions, science and technology, philosophy, and popular culture.

If you're writing a fantasy novel, should you read this book first to find out what fables are out there? What phrases may inspire you for your own novel? From 'Beauty and the Beast,' to beefcake, and beauty is only skin deep, to Frankenstein, and frankincense, and Freemason, and freeride, this fatty is designed to help every novelist discover words and phrases to beef up your writing.

Dictionary of English Synonyms and Antonyms

From Penguin

This revised edition of the existing *Nuttall's Dictionary of Synonyms and Antonyms* is designed to help widen the reader's and indeed the self-published writer's vocabulary.

The Penguin *Dictionary of English Synonyms & Antonyms* provides lists of synonyms, which are alternative words having the same meaning, while lists of antonyms provide words of opposite meaning.

So instead of being in a MUDDLE: Confusion, mix up, jumble, scramble, disorder, disarrangement, mess up. But take care in your writing so that you don't: Perplex, bewilder, confuse, confound, befuddle, stupefy - your readers.

Try dipping into this easy to navigate guide when you need to get your verbs jumping off the pages of your novel.

The Penguin Dictionary of English Idioms

By David Hinds-Howell, Daphne M Gulland

For a writing reference delight, try *The Penguin Dictionary of English Idioms*, with 4,000 plus idioms.

Another easy to read and navigate dictionary, this reference book looks at a range of examples, providing definitions and explaining how they should be used. A very practical guide, it is arranged by themes, making it possible to compare all the idioms in a particular subject area and find the right one for the occasion, whether in writing or speech.

So if you're a self-published author, don't ... GO DOWN WITH THE SHIP.

Instead - stay at one's post until the bitter end. As the guide explains, this phrase means: 'There was a tradition that the captain should go down with his ship. When the Titanic sank (1912), both the captain and designer went down with the ship, although they were offered places in the life-boats. In modern times, the rule has been relaxed, and the captain is expected to be the last to leave the ship.

Roget's Super Thesaurus

By Marc McCutcheon

This is your one-stop guide to synonyms, antonyms, vocabulary builders, and reverse lookups. Roget's has always been a writer's second hand, so this Roget's Super Thesaurus is a perennial favourite among writers.

This latest edition has more than 1,000 new and expanded entries. This time-saving reference will help you find the perfect synonym or antonym to give your writing precision and colour. From 'aback' to 'zydeco', you'll find the exact word you need.

You'll find this easy to use writing resource comprehensive in content, with reverse dictionary, sample sentences, enlightening quotes and more than 400,000 synonyms and antonyms. So the next time that elusive, just-right word or phrase is on the tip of your tongue, reach for *Roget's Super Thesaurus.*

With more features than any other word reference, it's a must-have for every writer's desk. Extremely useful and clean-looking, with easy reference points that make it easy to jump into the book and find words. However, although it is ideal for American writers, it would be great to have a UK version. Come on, *Writers Digest,* please do something similar for us 'English' Brits who also want this kind of super word reference!

So there you have it. A great list of the best Dictionaries and Thesauruses for Writers!

Look Out For ...

Digital dictionaries (next up), either online or downloaded to your PC, are great to have for looking up a quick reference.

Digital Dictionaries

A Web of Words

If you have an old paperback dictionary or thesaurus that's losing pages from all your thumbing through it to find synonyms and related words for your self-published novel, you'll need to check out a few Online Dictionaries.

And if, like me, you are frustrated with the limitations to the latest version of MS Word and its inability to use UK English, and its constant forcing of misspelt words on you, you'll love to know there is a great online dictionary with all the correct spellings for UK English.

WordWeb is a comprehensive one-click English thesaurus and dictionary for Windows. As you're writing, it takes only one click to look up words from almost any word processing program you prefer to use.

The one click gives you the word's definition as well as synonyms and related words to spice up your writing.

If you need pronunciations, you'll find them in *WordWeb*, along with usage examples that may spark off some new creative sentences to use in your self-published novel. Handy too is the sounds-like links, which also inspire new thought processes as you write.

You can use the free download, but I highly recommend buying *WordWeb Pro 7*. In addition to all the free version features, the full Pro version includes 5000 more definitions and numerous extra features. See more features of WordWeb: www.wordweb.info

I've used this fantastic little gem for years. It helps to enhance my writing by giving me a smorgasbord of words to choose from. I use it to check spellings where MS Word fails me. I use it to find out if words should be hyphenated or not. And I use it to find active verbs and check if I am using too many adjectives. And like this very paragraph - I 'use' it to avoid using the same word again and again. In my own writing I try to ensure that I never 'use' the same descriptive word twice - at least not on the same page. *WordWeb Pro* is the word bible that gives me peace of mind, knowing I have a wide choice of words at my fingertips.

Editing a Self-Published Novel

If you are editing your self-published manuscript, you can select a synonym in *WordWeb* and replace the look-up word with your newly chosen word. *WordWeb* has the option to highlight frequently used synonyms, great for helping you write clear, easy-to-understand English.

If you are keen on cutting down on word-clutter, *WordWeb* helps by showing you a particular part of speech. You can see if your word is an adverb and cut it out! Or you can shave down your use of adjectives when you realise that your word is one. Also, try clicking on the Noun, Verb, Adjective or Adverb buttons to show only the relevant synonyms and related words.

Browsing around to find related words is simple and helps to keep your writing tight by using powerful word replacements. In *WordWeb*, you just click on the tabs for synonyms, antonyms, parts, part of, types, type of, similar, see also, and anagrams.

WordWeb's extensive, up-to-date dictionary database features:

- Definitions and synonyms, including many compound and proper nouns
- Word relations: find antonyms, parts or types, less specific words, etc.
- Over 130 000 synonym sets and 163 000 root words
- Search over 280 000 words, compounds and derived forms
- 70 000 pronunciations, with pop-up hint pronunciation key
- 70 000 usage examples
- View alphabetically nearest words, suggestions for many misspellings

WordWeb Pro runs under Windows XP, Vista, Windows 7, Windows 8 (desktop) and Windows 10. You do not need to be online to use *WordWeb*, as it runs from your PC, but you can choose to go online and use one of the online dictionaries featured in this dictionary software.

Using Oxford English in Your Self-Published Novel

The *Oxford Dictionary of English* is at the forefront of language research, focusing on English as it is used today. This comprehensive reference is informed by the most up-to-date evidence from the largest language research programme in the world, including the 800-million-word *Oxford English Corpus*.

Within *WordWeb*, you can also get all the features of Oxford English, which includes:

- 350 000 words, phrases and meanings
- 67 000 usage examples
- 75 000 audio pronunciations
- 11 000 encyclopaedic entries
- 550 usage notes
- Word list of 280 000 entries for word finding and use with Crossword Compiler

Your Dictionary Mentor

The Dictionary tells us that Sage is 'aromatic fresh or dried grey-green leaves used widely as seasoning for meats and fowl and game.' It also means: A mentor in spiritual and philosophical topics who is renowned for profound wisdom.

In this case, *The Sage English Dictionary and Thesaurus* downloadable software for writers is your dictionary mentor that will guide your self-published books to profound wisdom.

The Sage English Dictionary and Thesaurus is another online dictionary that provides a comprehensive English dictionary and thesaurus that provides a number of useful and, in some cases, unusual search tools. Please take a look at the feature list and documentation for details.

The guys who created The Sage state that they are linguists. Their interest in offering their software is academic, not commercial, thus The Sage is free. Yippeee for writers!

The Sage allows you to look up words directly from most applications, offering multiple detailed definitions, each coupled with its own thesaurus. Find it here: http://bit.ly/1NJwhaj

Along with *WordWeb Pro*, I use The Sage constantly when I am writing. If differs in many ways from *WordWeb*, but it is equally as powerful at delivering a wide choice of related words to use in your writing materials.

Look Out For ...

There are lots of online reference guides and dictionaries. For instance, if you are writing a story that features someone in the US or UK army and want to see some of the words that character would use, you can Google for specialist dictionaries. The same goes for many different subjects.

Writing Tools

Writing Courses

There is a lot of learning needed to create a page-turning book full of suspense and intrigue, one that also makes the reader worry about the characters who are in conflict.

During the writing of my historical conspiracy thriller, *The Grotto's Secret*, I knew that I wanted to create suspense for my reader. I wanted the novel to race along so the reader couldn't put the book down. A comment from a reader that your book is a page turner is every author's dream.

That's when I spotted a writing course for children, which listed the 3 Cs as a learning module.

Writing Conflict, Contrast and Characters

I dived right in and signed up for the course. Not only because I wanted to learn how to write great novels for children, filled with action and adventure, but because I had already written several and was awarded with an honourable mention for two of my unpublished children's novels in the Writer's Digest writing competition.

Structuring Your Novel

When it comes to learning how to structure your novel that will give your readers the pace a thriller needs, you have to study novel structure.

Another writing course I took on *Writing for Young Adults* included a whole section on this. Because this course is so intense and detailed, and so extremely thorough and well planned, this kind of learning would be great for any aspiring novelist and writer. You will learn how to put all your planning and research and fictional character profiles together into a structure that will keep your readers turning the pages!

These courses are not just ideal for your manuscripts for children's stories, but also for any novel you want to write. The strategies really helped me to ensure that the structure of my historical conspiracy thriller, *The Grotto's Secret*, has all the elements and beats required to get cracking and whip my suspense story into shape.

If you want to learn how to create a great suspense conspiracy thriller that kicks butt, try taking a writing course like the ones I mentioned above. By signing up for a great writing course, you will have all the tools you need for creating exciting plots, vivid settings, and memorable characters. It is a serious must-do for all writers of Young Adult Fiction, Children's Fiction, and, in fact, any genre!

Scrivener Writing Software

Every aspiring writer, accomplished author, self-published author, and heck, even aspiring wannabe novelists have turned their thoughts to writing software at some point or other. If this is you, you need to know about a powerful writing tool ...

I'd heard a lot about Scrivener; mostly that it's a brilliant, flexible package for writers and authors to help manage the creative process from start to finish, keep all notes and research ideas grouped together and let the creative juices start flowing.

So I dived in and gave it a try.

If you're working on any material, from books to screenplays, and you feel frustrated with Word or whatever software you're using (maybe OneNote to keep your bits and bobs handy), you have just got to move over to Scrivener.

No matter what writing project you're in or on, it can be pretty scary to get to grips with all the work that is needed to hold your thoughts and wild imaginings together.

A complete novel or work of non-fiction takes plenty of time and mounds of planning, re-planning, shifting, re-ordering, editing and re-editing, and re-editing yet again before you see anything that can safely face the light of day - let alone be shown to an agent or publisher.

So where do you begin?

You could try the good old-fashioned software widely available on most PCs, or you could go Pro and break your project into manageable chunks.

I wish I'd had this powerful tool when writing both my books - *Create a Successful Website* and *Pimp My Site*; my writing life would have been soooooo much easier!

First and foremost, Scrivener gives you freedom to work on your project in segments, with two ways to work or view your work. Say hello to the corkboard and the outline view. Scrivener describes them as a bird's-eye view of your project segments.

Scrivener software helps you get far more organised than any note-taking app - I have used OneNote and have looked briefly at TreePad - but the flexibility of Scrivener gives you far more than just organisation and free flow writing.

The advanced ability to use tools such as the cork board for random ideas, and also to move chapters around, unbinds the chains of regular software and actually does what Red Bull is supposed to do - give you wings!

Talking of software and Word, Scrivener isn't a word processor per sé; it was designed to let writers tackle larger projects, gathering multiple documents, notes and research materials all in one place, allowing you to rearrange them at will - this is the beauty and freedom!

There are other writing software tools on the market, most of which are expensive and will take time to learn how to use.

Scrivener is easy to use with a few quick tutorials found on YouTube. Planning and research is easy to store and find in Scrivener.

Other Word Processing Software

What I liked about WPS Writer is that it has a familiar look to Microsoft Word with the same amount of innovative features. One thing I found quite quickly, which Microsoft Word does not have, is the ability to change the view to protect your eyes.

I spotted this in 'View,' and when selected, it dulls the screen and puts a soft greenish layer over the bright white to stop the glare. Most writers who spend countless hours in front of a glaring screen will know about eye strain and the resulting headaches. After using this for a month on the free trial, you will see the benefit WPS Writer offers an author.

Text Aloud

I often read my written work out loud to myself because it helps to spot typos and grammatical errors. When I Googled to see if there was software that could do this for me, I found TextAloud.

This dapper download reads text aloud from your email, web pages, marketing materials and any written work from your PC. It is ideally suited for people with limited eyesight, but is also a huge help in giving your marketing materials, and in particular your eBooks, a prime polishing. I now use it for press releases too.

TextAloud offers a free trial, and the voices don't sound too robotic. You can also purchase premium voices with English or American accents if you wish. Web owners and digital marketers will receive great value from this smart little tool.

See how you can avoid publishing your eBook and other articles with typos and errors by giving it a go at http://bit.ly/1QhvYSE

Dragon Naturally Speaking

Dragon NaturallySpeaking is speech recognition software that lets you speak your novel into your computer rather than typing it out.

This dragon turns spoken words into text and executes voice commands much faster than you can type, so you can plot away in your head while you speak into your computer's microphone as you dictate so that your manuscript is written wirelessly.

If you suffer from hand cramps or any other type of illness affecting your hands, you can stop typing and start speaking to get your novel published.

You can also switch between typing and voice, so you can use the mode of input you prefer for writing your novel.

After my self-edit of the final draft, I prefer to hear my novel read back to me. I find so many glitches in grammar and clumsy sentences by doing this. Even little things like hearing the voice just about gasping for breath helps me see where a comma should be inserted or the sentence rewritten.

Having your entire novel read back to you is an important step in self-editing. If you don't have someone with time on their hands and a wonderfully expressive voice, try getting TextAloud or DragonNaturallySpeaking to read your novel to you.

Look Out For ...

You can also use Microsoft's OneNote for keeping all your research and notes on a new novel together. It gives you a Word-type format where you can add sections which show up as 'tabs' and inside each section you can add more pages.

So for example, you could have one Notebook for your fantasy novel and then different tabs/sections for things like 'research,' 'characters,' 'plot' etc. And under each of these tabs you can add different pages; for example, under your 'research' tab, you can have different pages for different areas of research so it is all kept in one place but sectioned off so you can find things much easier.

You can also drop in a link to a document, add images, screen-shots and to do lists - I am BIG on to do lists!

I'm a bit eccentric really; I even add things to my list that I have already done, but that weren't there in the first place - JUST for the satisfaction of crossing them off again. Sad, hey? If you have this weird tendency, do drop me a line so I know there is someone else like me out there. (Smilie face).

One more thing: if you're an English UK writer and sick of Word not giving you the correct UK English language settings, try WPS Writer.

This looks and feels like Word with all Word's features, but is easy to set UK English as your default. The latest Office 365 also has this but doesn't have a UK English Dictionary built in so all your writing defaults to US English. Pretty damn annoying, I can tell you. Enough for me to leave Word after using it for most of my writing days.

WPS Writer also offers writers a great inside tool called 'Eye Protection Mode.' I am using this right now as I write because it prevents screen glare. If you're fixed on Word try going to the 'design' ribbon (not sure where this is in the older versions), and then in 'page background' you'll find 'page colour' where you can set the background to a light green shade to relieve that stark whiteness that can hurt your eyes after hours of writing.

Not The End

I hope you've enjoyed reading about these writing books, any of which will improve and spice up your writing.

As I have said before in this book, please do let me know if you have discovered an excellent writing book. Not only will I want to get my paws on it, but I would be more than happy to include a review from you and of course, give you a credit for sharing the book.

I have been writing for years, more than I care to count. I have never lost the vision that I will one day be a published novelist.

If I look back at my first novels (God forbid!) they are awful compared to my latest manuscripts. Even though I had a few agents back then telling me that I wrote well and could hold my reader in suspense, I knew I had to learn more and more about the craft of writing a page-turning novel.

When I received an 'Honourable Mention' in the 75th Annual Writers Digest Writing Competition for two novels I had written and not yet published, it spurred me on to learn the techniques and art of writing a great novel.

If you are lacking in some area of your writing, and you order one of the books listed here, I am sure you will itch impatiently until it has arrived.

Or, when it comes to the desire to learn a new writing technique, like me, with my impatient streak, you will download it straight onto your reading device and go curl up in a corner with a hot comforting drink and begin your adventure of reading to learn.

My family and friends have supported me in my dream, as I am sure yours do. If they don't, please don't lose heart. Never lose your dream! Keep your passion alive by reading a plethora of writing guides to nudge you along towards your writing career.

Almost all of us aspiring authors (and in fact thousands of accomplished authors too) will suffer doubt about their ability to be a published author.

Ignore those little devils sitting on your shoulder and believe the little angel sitting on the other side. You CAN write. You WILL write. One day your novel WILL be published. It's a long and winding road, but one that has to be taken in order to fine-tune your works of fiction.

Another idea to throw at you. Why not start a blog? It's as easy as baking an apple pie. Maybe even easier with the range of blogging platforms available today. My first book, *Create a Successful Website*, may help you there. But I am not saying this to merely flog my book.

It certainly helps being a professional writer. I am lucky to have that luxury. I have edited numerous online websites, including iHubbub's home business magazine and my own site called U Self-Publish, where I started to share my passion for learning to be a great writer.

You can blog about your writing life, maybe about the learning curve you're facing to be a novelist, or share some of the books you learn from and post reviews like I have done.

You may already blog about sewing, crafting cards or your latest diet, for all I know. The point is that writing in a professional capacity will help hone your writing while you read a batch of writing advice books to improve your stories. If you are skilled in a particular subject, you may even consider writing non-fiction books to get you a few steps ahead.

Although this is where we part ways, this is most definitely not the end for you or me.

Keep reading. Keep writing. Keep learning more techniques to weave through your novels. And keep pimping your fiction to impress readers with excellent writing techniques and transform your novels into page-turning bestsellers.

Above all, *always* treasure your vision to be a fiction author!

The End of
Pimp My Fiction

If you enjoyed reading *Pimp My Fiction*, please give me the gift of a review on Amazon. It doesn't have to be glowing, only genuine and fair. All you need to do is click the review link on this book's page on Amazon. Thank you for your support!

Read on for more books, acknowledgements, notes and bonus materials.

Writers' Resource Series

Powerful Writing Produces Bestsellers: Secrets of How to Write a Novel Using Techniques from the Best Reference Guides on Creative Writing

&

A~Z Writers' Character Quirks: Writers' A~ Z of Behaviours, Foibles, Habits, Mannerisms & Quirks for Writers to Create Fictional Characters

&

101 Writers' Scene Settings: Unique Location Ideas & Sensory Details for Writers to Create Vivid Scene Settings
Check for future editions: http://paulawynne.com/writers-resource-series

Bonus Material

1. Don't forget to pick up your FREE copy of *Pimp My Fiction* here:
   http://eepurl.com/bC336f

2. Join Paula Wynne's mailing list to receive the latest news about upcoming releases and specials just for subscribers:
   http://eepurl.com/byjPVT

If you stay on Paula's mailing list, you will be given the opportunity to get a free review copy of her next books.

3. Scenes Checklist: Download Paula's Scenes Checklist to create your scenes:
   http://eepurl.com/bC_vjX

4. Settings Checklist: Download Paula's Settings Checklist with sensory details for writers' to create vivid scene settings:
   http://eepurl.com/bC_vjX

5. Free sample chapters of *Pimp My Site*, *The Grotto's Secret* and *A~Z Writers' Character Quirks*:
   http://eepurl.com/byv2wT

Acknowledgements

I would like to express my gratitude to the authors who have given me permission to share my review of their books listed in *Pimp My Fiction*.

A special thank you to Rayne Hall, who wrote the foreword. I am honoured that she chose to have her esteemed name so closely associated with mine.

Many, many thanks to the successful authors who continue to help aspiring writers by sharing their knowledge in the craft of fiction writing.

About The Author

As an award-winning entrepreneur Paula Wynne has appeared on TV several times, including breakfast shows and has been featured in various magazines and national newspapers.

Paula and her husband Ken starred in the BBC Show, *Escape to the Continent*, which showed their quest to live in Spain so Paula could become a full time writer.

For many years Paula has been obsessed with learning everything to improve her writing. She has acquired a bookshelf of excellent reference books by highly acclaimed authors, so she wrote *Pimp My Fiction:* Secrets of How to Write a Novel. This inspired a Writers' Resource Series with *101 Writers' Scene Settings* and *A~Z Writers' Character Quirks*.

Paula received an 'Honourable Mention' in the 75th Annual Writers Digest Writing Competition for two unpublished novels.

Now Paula is really excited to be publishing her first novel, *The Grotto's Secret.*

19409740R00115

Printed in Poland
by Amazon Fulfillment
Poland Sp. z o.o., Wrocław